Library of Congress Copyright TX0008975380 2021
Hardback ISBN 978-1-0879-5631-2
Ebook ISBN 978-1-0879-5632-9

First Printing, 2021

Book design by Leah Ruth Blumer

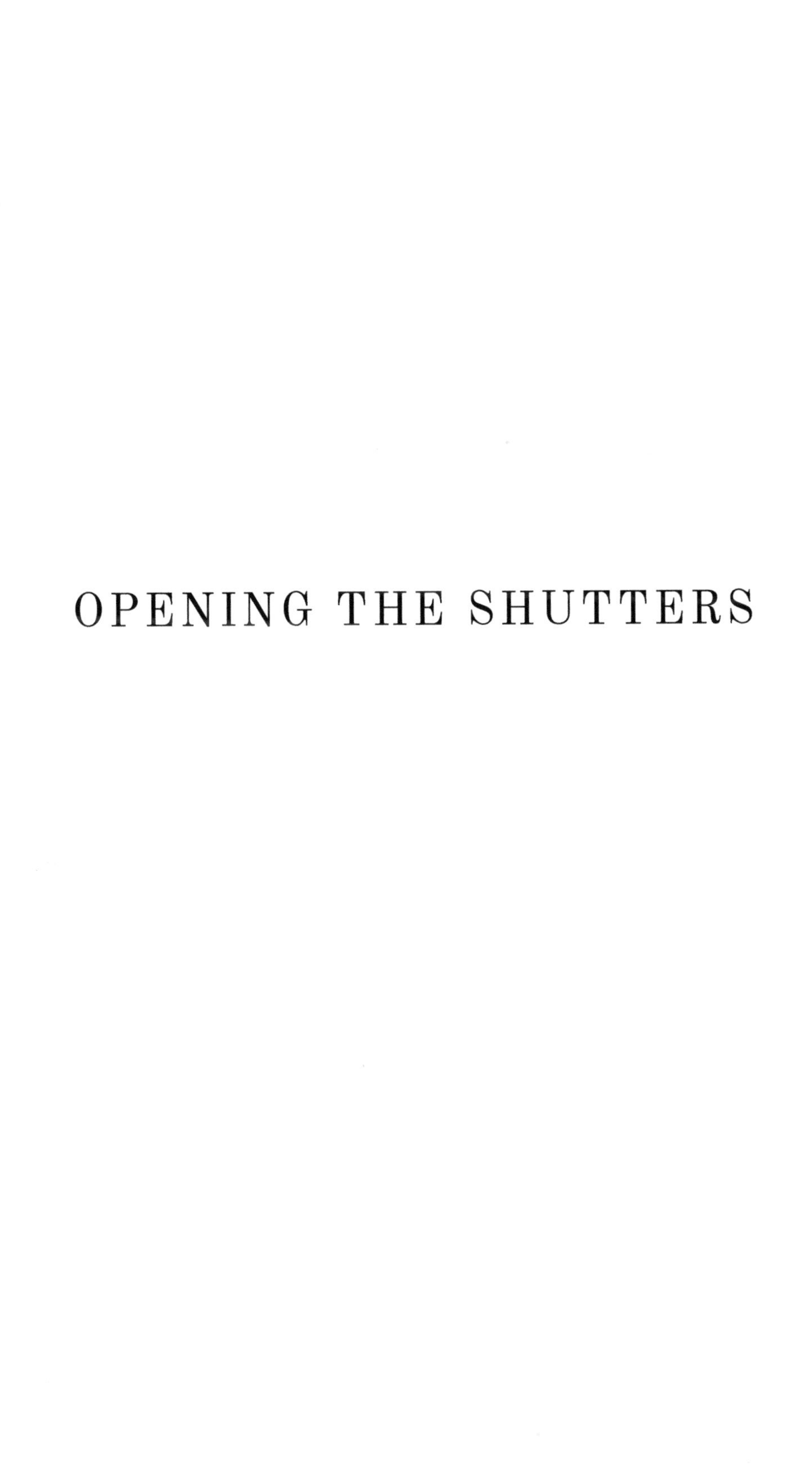

OPENING THE SHUTTERS

OPENING THE SHUTTERS

James A. Blumer

BlumCorr, LLC

Contents

1

Letting The Light In

In that overflowing storehouse called memory, my mind is filled with millions of files full of pictures, words, and recordings of procedures, sounds and sensations. Some memories are simply tools that I have acquired from birth onward throughout life to meet the needs for existing, making a living, and exercising my talents. Many of those files are also filled with my personal history and recollections. While some are buried in piles of rubbish and indistinct even when I can find them, I have many of these memories neatly filed away, plainly labeled and kept crystal clear. Even so, I never quite know what to expect when I open the shutters and let some light shine into the dim nooks and crannies.

I don't understand the rules that determine why I can recall certain things but not others. Some, of course, are easy to recall because they are so terrible. These are the ones that I would rather destroy, just as easily as a computer erases a file from memory upon command. But they appear to be indestructible, and they seem to be strategically placed. These memories I must look at whenever I search for anything that is related, either by chronology or content. Others are not blocked by any such obstacles. Neatly filed and plainly labeled, they make me feel good when I pull them out to look, read, listen, and feel.

And of course, there are those that seemingly have no particular significance at all. I just stumble over them unexpectedly when I am looking for something else.

From time to time, I have been sitting down to write whatever I come across when I open my storehouse. As anyone who has ever cleaned up an attic or a storage place knows, it is hard to decide what to keep and what to throw away. I will not apologize for cluttering the stories with details. As far as I am concerned, those details must be included in the chronicle if I am to present a true narrative. For example, stories of life on the farm in the second quarter of the twentieth century deserve to be told accurately lest they be forgotten or romanticized beyond recognition.

It is now time to put the pieces together to present my story. I would like to paint a background for the picture of my life, and that background is a view of the land of my childhood, and the people who populated it.

2

The Land

The glaciers that molded the terrain of northern Iowa, as well as most of the upper Midwest, left a deep layer of black topsoil. However, as the glaciers melted, they left a lot of rocks and gravel as well. Some large areas in this region are almost completely flat, except for shallow depressions and sluggish meandering streams. In fact, the Union Slough in Kossuth County is a geological curiosity. It is the remnant of a glacial riverbed. While it is at a higher elevation than the surrounding terrain, it is so flat that it may drain either north, into Minnesota, or south into Iowa depending on which way the wind is blowing!

Before the land was settled, prairie fires were a natural occurrence that prevented growth of trees except those that grew along the channels of the rivers and larger creeks. The prairie grasses formed a tough sod that thrived despite floods and fires.

Early pioneers recognized that this terrain had the potential for being excellent farmland. Even before the railroads arrived in this part of Iowa, entrepreneurs interested in developing the area employed a floating dredge, powered by steam, which worked its way up the Boone valley from central Iowa toward Minnesota.

The coming of the railroads transformed the prairie lands from a frontier into an agricultural area, bringing in a flood of settlers, many of whom were immigrants who had recently arrived in this country.

Many of the small towns in the Midwest were established at the time the railroads were built, located wherever the steam locomotives needed to make a water stop. The location of the town of LuVerne, Iowa was determined by the fact that two railroads crossed there. The railroads reached this junction about 1879. Each railroad built a water tank and depot, and within a short time the town grew up in the mile between the two stations.

The early settlers in this flat prairie faced a huge job of draining sloughs and potholes before they could farm much of the land. They also had to remove the rocks. The glacial deposits were littered with granite boulders. Farmers used a lot of dynamite to break the larger boulders into chunks that were small enough to be moved by horses or picked up by hand. The enormous task of draining the land started in the late 19th century when the first settlers moved in, and it continues to some extent even today. It was accomplished first by surface drainage, although most of that activity was finished about the time of World War I. Ponds and sloughs were drained by digging ditches. Many of the smaller ditches were dug by hand or with teams of horses pulling scrapers. I remember my Dad talking about bull teams-- twenty or more bulls hitched to a huge plow that plowed a ditch across the prairie. Larger ditches were excavated by steam shovels. Along with digging ditches to drain the swamps, it became necessary to deepen and straighten the natural watercourses that meandered eventually into the Des Moines River.

Our farm was located on this flat prairie, in Kossuth County Iowa, which is near the middle of the northern tier of counties bordering on Minnesota. When I was growing up on the farm, the first phase of drainage of the prairies was history. There was already an elaborate underground drainage network in place. All the underground drains were known by the generic name of "tile." This term is still in use. It is derived from the hard-fired clay pipes or tiles that were used. These were made from the same type of clay as building bricks. They are extremely durable, and many of the tiles laid 75 or more years ago are still working. Unless they are crushed by heavy machinery, they may be expected to last 100 years or more in the ground. The main drains were financed by county governments and are still maintained through taxes. They are built of tile anywhere from twelve inches up to four feet or more in diameter. Each farm owner installed branch tile to drain wet areas, and these tiles usually flow into the county drains. The laterals or branch tile are usually five or six inches in diameter. The tile networks were never expected to prevent flooding caused by heavy rains. Rather, the objective was to dry the land enough that it could be cultivated during seasons of normal or moderately heavy rainfall, and to drain away standing water quickly enough to prevent drowning of crops. Inevitably, some crops are drowned out in low places when heavy rains fall, for the drainage system cannot handle the peak loads quickly. Typically, it takes three days to a week to drain all the surface water after a heavy rain. Most tiles depend entirely on taking in water through the soil. Intakes, which allow surface water to flow directly into the tile, are used only where large quantities of water collect.

3

Historical Background

Many of the small towns in the Midwest were established at the time the railroads were built, located wherever the steam locomotives needed to make a water stop. The location of the town of LuVerne, Iowa was determined by the fact that two railroads crossed there. The railroads reached this junction about 1879. Each railroad built a water tank and depot, and within a short time the town grew up in the mile between the two stations.

4

My Family

My Father, Paul Blumer (1886-1980)

Among the first residents of the rural community surrounding LuVerne were my grandparents, Swiss immigrants who came to north central Iowa in 1880 to join a few other Swiss families who lived in southern Kossuth County and northern Humboldt County near the towns of LuVerne and Renwick. They settled on a farm in Kossuth County, near the town of LuVerne, and farmed in the same locality until they retired in 1907.

I was born December 10, 1927, the youngest of four boys in the family. My older brothers are Ralph, John, and Philip. We lived on a farm in section 16, Sherman Township, Kossuth County, Iowa. My parents moved to the farm shortly after they were married in 1918 and lived there until they retired and moved to LuVerne in the early 1950's.

I never really knew either of my grandmothers because they both died before I was old enough to remember them. After he retired from farming, my grandfather, John Blumer, lived in Renwick, Iowa, about twenty miles from our farm. I remember Grandpa only as a little old man with a long gray beard who spoke only Swiss German. I understand that he could speak English, but when Dad talked to him, they only conversed in German. Since I never learned any German, I never talked to him. Most of the times I remember being around him at all is when we went to visit him in the Old People's Home in Cedar Falls, Iowa, where he lived the last few years of his life.

My other grandfather was never in the picture at all. He deserted my grandmother and their three young children when my mother was a small child. She would never mention him at all and refused to answer any questions concerning him. In fact, we never learned anything about him while my mother was alive. My brothers, Ralph and Phil, the genealogy experts in our family, spent years tracing our maternal grandfather after our mother died. The name he used while he was married to my grandmother was Charles Emrie. He led an interesting if not exactly honorable life. He was a Civil War veteran who fought with the Union Army in several of the lesser-known battles of the war. While he was originally from Pennsylvania, he moved to Kansas after the war, married and fathered a family of six children. He deserted them and vanished without a trace for many years. For most of the rest of his life he was successful in concealing his first marriage while he traveled about the country working as a stonecutter.

Eventually he turned up in Iowa and met and married my grandmother, concealing the fact that he was already married. They had three children. Then, exactly as he had done before in Kansas, he left their home on the pretext of going to the store and instead boarded a train and vanished. Since he used several different names and moved from state to state many times, putting the pieces of his life history together was a major project. In fact, it was only in the 1990's, over sixty years after my grandmother's death, that Phil finally learned the old rascal's real name and was able to account for most of his life history. The War Department records finally revealed some of the missing pieces of the puzzle.

His first wife, having heard nothing from him for seven years, had him legally declared dead and began collecting the widow's pension provided to widows of Civil War veterans. Years later, after he deserted his Iowa family, my grandmother resorted to legal procedures as well. Knowing nothing of the veteran's first wife, but having enough information to contact the War Department, she likewise applied for the widow's pension. She was shocked when her request was denied because someone was already collecting the pension. Finally, the veteran himself, then living in Pennsylvania, decided to retire. He applied for his soldier's pension and discovered that he was dead according to the War Department records. The War Department sent an auditor to interview him and stored the auditor's report in the archives. The report supplied some of the missing information and finally confirmed our grandfather's true identity. In a final irony, he then went back to Kansas and moved in with his first wife for the last year of his life. Those are the bare facts of the story, but there are still missing pieces. There are years of his history that are still blank. We do not know where he was or the alias he was using at those times. For all we know he may have had other wives and children. We will never know if our mother knew of the other family. The only comment I ever heard from someone who actually knew him came from my mother's cousin. When she was very old, but still mentally sharp, she told me, *"Your grandfather was a very handsome man"*.

Before I went to school, I never played with any other kids except my three brothers. We went to church every Sunday, so I knew a few kids that I saw only in church and Sunday school, but we had no contact with them outside of the church. When I write about it, it sounds like a lonely existence, but I never felt that way. Probably that is why I have never minded being alone. In fact, I like having quite a bit of solitary time. Incidentally, the kids I knew in church were mostly members of the Marty clan, who like the Blumers, came originally from Canton Glarus, Switzerland. In fact, my grandmother Blumer was a Marty.

Boredom was a word that was not even in my vocabulary when I was growing up on the farm. There was always something to do. Every day, there was work to be done and playtime was often snatched away from time when I could have been doing some useful task if I had wanted to do so. Of course, when school was in session, I could play at recess with the other kids in the neighborhood, but my brothers were my only companions at home. Ralph and John were the big boys, and Phil and I were the little boys. The age difference between the two pairs of boys had a lot to do with our relationship. When I was six or seven or eight years old, if you had asked me to describe Ralph and John, I probably would have said they were mean and rough. There can be no doubt that they were a couple of tough kids, but that was because the hardships of the worst years of the depression affected their lives severely, while Phil and I had a little easier time of it. All four of us honed our survival skills early in life because we grew up having to face harsh realities. We had only limited opportunities to acquire social skills outside of our family. For that reason, there is no point in comparing us with kids that are growing up now. Ralph was the toughest of the bunch, and he and I fought a lot. John was not as hard on us, but if provoked enough he would get rough with us little boys, although he never hit us hard enough to seriously hurt us. He and Ralph really knew no other way to resolve conflicts so the two of them had a lot of bloody battles. I know now that the same could be said about Phil and me. We fought each other a lot, and when I say fight, I mean we used our fists. I don't know about Phil, but I know that I usually hit as hard as I could. We outgrew the habit of fighting as we grew older and as adults we have always gotten along very well.

5

The Old House

Early childhood memories are hard to sort out. They are indistinct bits of recollection, and even then, there is always a doubt. Is this something that I really remember, or is it something I heard about later? I remember very little of my early childhood before the fall of 1932. For me, the event that divides real memories from those doubtful ones is the day when our old house burned to the ground. It was truly a life-changing event that is indelibly engraved in my memory.

I cannot recollect much about life in the old house. I do know I played outside a lot and was very familiar with the other buildings on the farm. I knew all the horses by name and spent a lot of my time tagging along with my dad and my older brothers as they did the daily chores. Our farm buildings were a quarter mile from the mailbox where our lane joined the county road. Getting the mail was one of the big events of the day. The Des Moines Register was our daily paper. It was delivered by our mail carrier along with our other mail. We had the weekly Algona Advance for our local news and those two newspapers were our connection to the outside world. I learned to read when I was four and was reading the newspapers before I went to school.

We did not have electricity then, but we had a telephone in the old house. It was the classic wooden box mounted on the wall with a crank to ring the operator or anyone on our party line. Everyone on the line had a distinctive combination of long and short rings. The universal code for an emergency was a very long continuous ring. The line was a single wire attached to little poles, mounted on blue glass insulators. Long distance calls were highly unusual, and generally reserved for extreme emergencies such as a death in the family.

Every family had a car by the time I came along. I know that Dad once had a 1923 Model T Ford, but I don't know if that was his first car or not. I believe he bought it new. The earliest one I remember was a 1926 Model T Ford. We lived five miles from LuVerne and twelve miles from Algona, so the car saved a lot of time when we had to go to town. Why were the car and the telephone important? They were links that connected us to the community. Never were those links more important than when disaster struck such as it did the day our house burned down.

In October 1932, I was almost five years old. Being the youngest child in the family, I was the only kid at home during school hours. Two of my brothers, Phil and John, were attending country school, and the oldest, Ralph, was enrolled in high school in Algona. It was "corn picking time" on the farm. That was one of the busiest times of the year, when every able-bodied man and some of the women and children too, were out in the cornfields harvesting the crop. A team of horses, controlled by voice commands, pulled a wagon while the picker walked alongside, stripping the husks off the ripe ears of corn, snapping the ears off the stalks, and throwing the ears into the wagon.

The house we lived in was old. It was the first house to be built on the farm, and it was not very big when it was first built, which was probably in the 1880's. At least one addition had been added later. By 1932, the house that was of rather haphazard frame construction and not very conveniently arranged to begin with, was showing its age and was not a very comfortable place to live. I remember very little of life there, but I have heard a great deal about it.

I will never forget the day our house burned. It was a bright, dry sunny day with a strong wind blowing out of the northwest. It was late in October, and there was already a chill in the air. Most of the leaves had fallen from the trees, and the wind was whipping the rest of the branches bare and drifting the leaves into piles here and there. It was cool enough that some heat was needed in the house, and my mother had built a fire in the heating stove. Of course, she always had a fire in the kitchen range for cooking. Aside from the fact that it was one of the coolest days of the season, that day started out to be just another typical fall day.

Dad came in from the field at noon, as always, unloaded his load of corn and ate dinner. Immediately after dinner, he hitched up the team again and headed for the field. After my mother had washed the dinner dishes, she apparently wanted to fix something, because she asked me to get the hammer for her. The claw hammer was probably used more than any other tool on the farm, and I knew exactly what she wanted and also knew where to look for it. I ran to the corncrib, which was located northeast of the house. I did not find the hammer and returned to the house, reporting that I could not find it. She went with me back to the corncrib to look for herself, but the hammer was not there. The next place to look was in the machine shed, which was south and a little east of the corncrib, almost directly east of the house. The machine shed had big sliding doors on the east side, rather hard for a little boy to open, so she opened a door, and I ran inside and found the hammer She closed the door and we started to walk back around the south end of the shed, toward the house. I was the first to see the fire.

The wind had drifted a pile of leaves into a valley on the northeast side of the roof of the house, and in that pile of leaves a fire was burning furiously. Obviously, a spark from the chimney had started the fire. It was small when I first saw it, not more than three feet across, but spreading fast in the dry leaves. I started yelling and pointing, trying to get my mother's attention. When she saw the fire, she ran back to the house, with me following as fast as my legs would carry me. The first thing she did was race to the old wooden telephone on the wall, crank it furiously and yell that our house was on fire. She then started to grab things and carry them outside. She yelled at me to go out to the field and get Dad. I was old enough to know my way around the farm buildings very well, but my knowledge of the fields was still a little vague. I knew that Dad was picking corn in the north field. My problem was that while I knew which direction to go, I did not know the best way to get there.

There were two fields of standing corn north of the house, one that started only a hundred yards north of the buildings and extended north about a fifth of a mile, and another adjoining it on the north that extended for another half mile. Unfortunately, I went into the nearest field first. None of the corn in that field had been picked and once into the corn I could not see anything more than a few feet away. The corn stood six feet high, and I wasn't very big. I followed the rows though and before long I came to the fence that divided the fields. I had a terrible time getting over the fence. It was called a hog tight fence and there was no way to get through it. I had to climb over the top. I finally got over the fence and into the other field, but then I didn't know how to find Dad. It was a very big field, and I couldn't see him anywhere. After looking for a few minutes, I decided to go home. In retrospect, it was probably a good thing I did. Finding a wagon in a half-mile long field of standing corn was a tough job for a four-year old. I might have looked for a long, long time.

When I turned back toward the farm buildings, I saw a huge cloud of black smoke rising into the air and being blown toward the southeast. If I had known how to find it, there was a lane out to the field and I need not have climbed any fences at all, but I chose to go back the way I came. I had an even worse time climbing over the fence than I did the first time because my clothing got caught in the barbed wire and I started to cry. That was the only time I cried during the whole ordeal. I really got scared then until I managed to work my clothes free of the fence, climbed over and started running back towards the house.

I could not see anything until I emerged from the cornrows at the end of the barnyard. The whole yard seemed to be full of cars. Pieces of furniture were scattered around, and people were standing and watching the fire. I made my way quite close to the house. By that time the whole interior was a roaring mass of flame. The roof was gone but some of the walls were still standing on the windward side. As I watched, the last curtains on the windows on the west side caught fire. They only burned for a moment, just a "poof," and they were gone. I could feel the heat searing my face even though I was standing some distance away.

I was so scared I was shaking, but I didn't cry. About that time someone spotted me standing there and picked me up and carried me to a safer place. I caught a glimpse of my mother. She was sitting in the back seat of Carl Swanson's car. Apparently, she had fainted or been overcome by smoke. Someone was holding wet cloths against her forehead. The man who picked me up set me down by a car and told me to sit there. I was at the edge of the crowd and could not see much of what was going on from there, and nobody paid any attention to me. I was sitting against the wheel of the car, and I remember looking at the wheel. It was not a model T Ford like I was used to. It had a rather heavy wheel with wooden spokes and a hubcap that was sort of cylindrical in shape with a larger ring on the outer end. I remember wondering whose car it was. There were many people there that I did not know, and nobody talked to me until Carl Swanson came to take me away.

While all of this was going on, Dad was picking corn, working his way north through the field, almost three-quarters of a mile away with his back toward the farm buildings. One of the neighbors drove his car out to the field and went to tell Dad. I remember hearing later that when Dad turned around and saw the smoke, he didn't even stop to get on the wagon. He left the team standing there and started to run home. The neighbor drove him back to the house, but by the time they got there, nothing could be done. The house burned completely, not leaving a stick undamaged. The fire did not spread to any other buildings although the intense heat did set some of the trees closest to the house on fire. The fire truck from LuVerne answered the call but, by the time they got there, there was nothing left but ashes. I remember hearing later that from the time the fire really became intense, the house burned down in twenty minutes.

My mother and the first neighbors to arrive managed to carry out some things before the roof fell in. Mike Stripling threw some of the things out of the second-floor windows. No one was hurt in the fire except that my mother was briefly overcome by smoke inhalation.

When people started to leave, Carl Swanson put me in his car and took me to the Swanson farm to spend the night. The next day Phil and I went to stay with Uncle Paul, (Paul Emrie, my mother's brother). Nobody told me anything about what was going on. I stayed with Uncle Paul and Aunt Ethel for at least two weeks. She was very good to me although I know I must have been an awful nuisance, because I kept wetting my pants. The next time I went back to the farm, the machine shed had been converted into a place to live. That was our dwelling for the next three years.

The loss of the old house was a blow to the whole family. It was not that any of us had any sentimental attachment to it. My mother hated the old house. It was dilapidated, uncomfortable and unhandy, and as far as back as I can remember she never had anything good to say about it. It was just that there was no practical way to replace it immediately, and we certainly didn't need any more troubles to add to those we already had. The Great Depression was at its worst during that time. The prices of farm products were so low that the farm produced almost no net income. We were subsisting on the food we could grow ourselves, with very little money to buy clothing, shoes, and other necessities.

The fire occurred in the midst of the corn harvest, which in those days was hand labor. "Corn picking time" started about the last week of September and dragged on until December most years. The threat of bad weather was always present. More years than not, winter had arrived before the last of the corn was picked. It was absolutely necessary for Dad to arrange some shelter for us immediately and get back to corn picking as soon as possible. Within a few days, Dad, with whatever help he could get, installed a wooden floor in part of the machine shed, which was really the only building on the farm which was at all suitable for conversion to a dwelling. They cut windows in the walls and installed barn sash, and boarded up the big doorways in front that were designed to move the machinery in and out. They moved in the few articles of furniture salvaged from the fire that would fit in the shed, and we moved in. To me, it seems as though I spent most of my childhood living in the shed, although I realize now that it wasn't that long. It certainly was an experience to remember, though. It was small, bare, cold in the winter and hot in the summer. In nice weather and often when it wasn't so nice, we kids spent as much time as possible outdoors. Of course, we always had chores to do every night and morning. Dad and all of us boys spent a large portion of our time in the neighboring barn during the colder months.

The shed was divided into small rooms. The interior partitions as well as the interior surfaces of the outside walls were covered with Celotex board. This is a soft, fuzzy product that was used for decades as sheathing under exterior siding in houses and other buildings. It is not practical to finish it in any way, so all our walls had the same drab brown appearance. Neither electricity nor running water was available on our farm at that time. We used kerosene lamps for light, with the added small luxury of an Aladdin lamp to brighten up our main room. The Aladdin was a lamp that used a kerosene flame to heat a mantle to white heat, giving off a much brighter, and whiter light than the regular kerosene lamps. When we went out to do chores in the dark, we used kerosene lanterns for light. Of course, there was always danger of fire from the lamps and lanterns, so we learned at a very early age to be careful, particularly in the barn, where there was highly inflammable hay and straw everywhere.

A potbelly stove was our main source of heat in the shed. For cooking and additional heat, we had a range in the kitchen. In the kitchen range, we burned corncobs almost exclusively. In the potbelly stove, cobs were used to start the fire and for quick heat, and in cold weather, coal was the main fuel. We burned a little wood, but not much in proportion to the number of cobs and coal. One memorable winter, the winter of 1933-34, we even burned some ear corn in the stove. It was moldy corn, not good for livestock feed, and it was certainly cheaper than coal. It burned very hot and fast and made a lot of snapping and crackling noise as it burned. As soon as the moldy corn was used up, we stopped burning corn, and never did it again. Even though corn was very cheap, it was against a thrifty farmer's principles to burn a crop that could be sold or fed to livestock.

Water for kitchen and household use had to be carried from the well in pails. This was one of the tasks that we kids had to start doing at an early age. The other thing that we always had to do was bring in corn cobs for fuel from a pile outside. I was expected to keep the cob basket full when I was about five years old. Of course, as I got older, other duties were added, but being the youngest, I had to carry in cobs for a long time. As I got older, I got to use a bigger pail to carry water, but that was also a never-ending chore. Often the windmill was running or just had to be turned on to pump the water, but there were plenty of times that there wasn't enough wind, or it just wasn't worthwhile to hook up the windmill to pump a pail of water, so it had to be pumped by hand. In cold weather, there was nothing colder than that old cast iron pump handle. In fact, in below zero weather it was dangerous to touch the pump handle with bare hands, for wet skin would immediately freeze to the cold iron.

6

The New House

In 1935, Dad built a new house. This was another landmark in my childhood, to be sure. I followed every detail of the construction, for the house was built during the summer so I was not in school at all during that time. A team of horses pulled a scraper to excavate the hole for the basement. That took care of most of the volume of dirt but left a lot of digging to do by hand. Our family did all the excavation. Dad hired some men to help build forms for the basement walls out of boards. We all helped mix the sand, cement and water and pour the concrete.

The carpenters who built the house were the Endahl brothers, Andy and Pete. They were Norwegians and spoke with heavy accents. They were fine craftsmen and were careful with every detail. There was no skimping whatsoever on the construction, for while the Endahls were thrifty and never wasted a piece of lumber if it could possibly be avoided, they knew very well what was required if the house was to be sturdy and straight. There were some innovations in the house. The walls were insulated with rolls of rock wool, something that was just beginning to be done in those days. Electric wiring and water pipes were enclosed in the walls, even though the Rural Electrification Administration was still widely considered an impractical dream. Otherwise, the construction was traditional. The interior walls were plastered, and the interior woodwork was oak on the ground floor and fir upstairs. The floors were all oak. It had a full basement and a coal-burning furnace. There was a big kitchen, a dining room, and a very large living room on the ground floor, and four bedrooms and a bathroom on the second. It was a very attractive and comfortable house, certainly a contrast from the shed where we lived before. I remember hearing that the house cost $4000, a lot of money in 1935.

There was time for play of course, but I really don't remember much of that part of life. I do remember that my favorite place to play was in the grove, the thick belt of trees that sheltered the farm buildings on the west and north sides. Many of the trees in the grove were huge cottonwoods, but there were also plenty of smaller trees for climbing. One of my favorite retreats was in a plum thicket that was so dense that when I cleared a space in the middle of it, I had created a haven than no one else knew about other than my brother Phil. It was accessible only by crawling through a sort of tunnel, through the bushes, that was so small it was hardly noticeable. I spent many hours in there playing with homemade toy tractors and trucks. I liked to play by myself a lot, but Phil and I also played a lot together.

7

The Bicycle

When I was a little older, old enough to ride a bicycle, life was a lot more enjoyable. Phil and I bought a bicycle in 1937. We regarded it as our most valuable possession. We had been given some chickens to raise, and when we sold them and got the money, almost twenty dollars, we immediately ordered the bicycle from Montgomery Ward. It was their basic no-frills Hawthorne model. It cost $17.95, but it was worth every penny. It was blue, and it had fat tires. It was heavier than bicycles are today, but it was durable, as it needed to be, for it was used every day except in the winter when snow and ice prevented riding. Much of the time it carried both of us. To do that, I sat sidesaddle on the frame ahead of the seat and held my legs out to the side to clear the pedals. We became skilled bicycle mechanics. We always took the coaster brake apart to clean and oil it, and kept the bearings oiled and properly adjusted. We rode it everywhere, including a lot of places we weren't supposed to. We rode it to country school much of the time and rode it to the mailbox to get the mail, which saved a lot of time, as the mailbox was a quarter of a mile from the house. It was a very practical way to get around.

8

Water

The well was the activity center for a lot of the daily chores, for it was the only source of water on the farm, aside from an underground cistern, which collected rainwater that was used for washing. The soft water from the cistern was clean enough for washing our hands and washing clothes but was not used for anything else. All the drinking water for the livestock, too, had to come from the well.

Running water came to the farm before electricity was available. This was accomplished by installing a force pump, which was capable of pumping water at high pressure. It was powered by the windmill or by a cranky old gas engine when the wind refused to blow. The engine was an old relic, a one-cylinder McCormick with two spoked flywheels. It frequently refused to start, and when it was running, alternately picked up speed, then wheezed a while as though it was dying, then came to life and popped until it had picked up speed again and repeated the cycle. This type of engine is known as a hit-and-miss engine. The pump worked very well, though. The storage tank was in the basement of the house. It held enough so that when the pressure was pumped up, there was enough water for a day or more of use. The only problem with it was that there was no way to start and stop it automatically. Someone had to start the pump when the water was low and watch the pressure and shut it off when it was high enough. Since it often took several hours to pump up enough pressure, it was very easy to forget. When that happened, the pressure relief valve on the tank would open and blow a blast of water across the basement, drenching everything within range. Then of course the tank had to be filled again. The other possibility when the pressure got too high was that the pump rod on the windmill would break. That happened a few times too.

Installation of the pressure system did not help with the livestock chores. Even after the pressure system was installed for the house, every drop of water for the chickens and the hogs, as well as calves and other cattle that were kept separate from the main herd, had to be carried in pails or hauled in a barrel. The stock tank was still filled by gravity through a pipe from the pump. That took care of the main herd of cattle and horses. Much of the time the horses were kept in the barn rather than allowed to run loose, so they had to be led out to the tank to drink. Most of the time, we used five-gallon pails to carry water. Each full pail weighed about forty pounds, so carrying two of them was work for a grown man, and a task for children that took every bit of strength they had. In the winter, all the water for the hogs was carried by hand and poured into open troughs for them to drink. We used a barrel on a skid made of planks in the summer when the hogs were on pasture. The skid had to be pulled by a team of horses or a tractor. Normally all the livestock had to be watered twice a day. Wet pant legs were the normal condition, rain or shine, cold weather or hot, because you could not carry and pour water without splashing some on yourself.

9

Daily Chores

There were always other chores to do also, such as feeding the chickens and gathering the eggs. These were also jobs that I was assigned at a very early age, and I hated them thoroughly. It certainly wasn't that there was anything difficult about it, it was just that I could always think of several things that I would rather be doing. I would hate to guess how many times I got spanked for rebelling at the daily job of "getting the eggs." Sometimes I think that would happen almost every day. Of course, getting in trouble was standard operating procedure for me.

Feeding the animals was another twice-daily task during most of the year. It was easy in the summer because the cattle were on pasture and the hogs needed only to have the feeders filled, a wagonload at a time, once or twice a week. Quite often, too, the sows were moved into the hog lot while the weaned pigs were on pasture, so they were fed corn directly from the crib, a matter of filling a bushel basket or two and scattering the ears in the hog lot.

Unfortunately, the summer lasted only about three months and for the rest of the year the cattle had to be fed regularly. As a matter of fact, the milk cows were fed a little grain at milking time throughout the year. This was another job that I started doing at a very early age. For some reason, I really didn't mind doing it. It was one chore that was ok.

Many of the rest of the livestock chores were sheer drudgery. Feeding hay was another job that I never objected to particularly, although the dust and chaff always bothered me. It was hard work, for the hay was hard to pull loose from the stack in the hayloft, or haymow as we called it. The settling, particularly in the layers closer to the floor, packed the hay together so tightly that it was difficult to pick apart. The only practical way to do it was to peel the layers of hay in the same order in which they were laid down. We used three-tine pitchforks for handling hay. As we pulled the hay loose in the haymow, we carried it over to a chute and threw it down to the ground floor. From there, it had to be distributed to the cattle and horses.

Milking the cows by hand was one of the most arduous tasks that had to be done every night and morning. I had to start milking when I was about seven and was assigned a certain cow that I was expected to milk. Later as I grew up, I had to milk more. I was never very good at it and, quite frankly, I didn't want to improve. It was a job I detested. It wasn't that I didn't like cows. Except for milking by hand, I really enjoyed working with them. Of course, milking had its own set of hazards. As you sat on your little one-legged milk stool with your head pressed against the cow's flank, you could expect to get slapped by the cow's tail. That was bad enough when the tail was dry, and quite often it wasn't. Then there was the ever-present danger of getting kicked. Some cows were gentle and hardly ever kicked, although even the most docile cow was likely to lift her leg and stick her hoof in the milk pail occasionally. Some cows were likely to kick at the slightest provocation, or for no apparent reason at all. A cow like that was dangerous. A kicking cow often gives no warning and the kick is fast and powerful. The person milking the cow was always in a vulnerable position. In fact, you were lucky if you were kicked completely clear of the cows. It was a lot worse if you were knocked down and stepped on. Of course, you were almost always sitting between two cows, so you were at risk from both the cow you were milking and the one behind you. It was possible to get quite badly hurt, although usually the only result was a few bruises and a job of cleaning up the milk pail.

10

Horses

Horses occupied a unique position in the scheme of things in those days. They were not pets, although they all were named, and each had a personality of its own. They were essential before the days of tractor farming, for the farm could not be worked without them.

Occasionally horses could be dangerous, too. A runaway team was always a possibility, and many farmers were seriously maimed in runaways, if not killed. In our own neighborhood there were two retired farmers who had one leg apiece. Their other legs were mangled in a runaway and had to be amputated.

These were big horses, some of them weighing over a ton apiece. Even the smallest of the horses we had weighed 1400 or 1500 pounds. They were strictly draft horses. Some of the smaller ones could be ridden but usually only kids at play would attempt to ride them. The bigger horses had such wide backs it was almost impossible to straddle them. Back when Dad farmed entirely with horses, he usually had eight, I believe. Even after he bought a tractor in the fall of 1937, he kept the horses and used them for much of the farm work. My favorite horses, which were the ones I usually drove, were a pair of grays. Their names were Prince and Queen. Prince was the biggest horse I remember having on the farm. Queen was a little smaller, but they were close enough to the same size to be a good team. They were both extraordinarily quiet and gentle. I do not know what breed they were or if they were of mixed breeds. They were both a solid light gray in color, very heavily muscled, with heavy necks. Prince used a very large collar. In fact, the only collars I have ever seen that are bigger are those used by the big Budweiser Clydesdales. The only time I can recall weighing the team, they weighed 4200 pounds together with their harness on. Their hoofs were, without exaggeration, as big as a dinner plate.

I was six or seven when I first began working with horses, other than driving the horses as we were loading hay, which I started at five. Soon after that I graduated to working with a team all by myself, cultivating corn with a single row cultivator. I was too small to harness the horses at that time, although before long I was expected to buckle up the harness after someone else threw it over the horse's back. Even after I was big enough to do it all by myself, harnessing Prince and Queen required some special tactics. Prince didn't like to have the bridle put on and would raise his head when he saw me coming with the bridle. He was so big I couldn't even reach his nose when he did that, so I would have to crawl up and stand on the hay manger in his stall to get the bridle on. He never tired of playing that game as long as I worked with him. Another thing he loved to do was step on my foot. He would watch for his chance, usually while I was putting on his collar, and deliberately pick up that huge front hoof and plant it on top of my foot. He never put much weight on it, for if he had he would have crushed my foot, but just let it rest there while I unsuccessfully tried to get my foot free and yelled at him and beat on him with my fists. Pretty soon he would pick up his hoof and let me go, but he never hurried. Those two were the only horses I ever really trusted in my life, and even now I remember them with real affection.

11

Tractor Farming

Those of us who grew up on a farm during the years of the Great Depression and World War II experienced a profound change in the way we lived when we began the conversion from dependency on horses to farming with a tractor. Part of the pressure that brought about this change came from those national and world events, and part of it was simply acceptance of the technology that enabled mechanization of the farm. Regardless of the cause, it was a time of emancipation from drudgery for farm families. I suspect that it is difficult for a non-farmer to understand the regard that our generation has for the old machines that made this transition possible. Perhaps I can contribute a tiny bit toward understanding the phenomenon by presenting the story of the transition from horse farming to machinery from my experiences.

Clearly, there were many demands for power beyond what men and horses could conveniently supply. The steam traction engines and the huge early tractors were well suited for breaking the tough prairie sod. However, in most cases, the land had to be drained first, and the rocks were still a formidable obstacle for plows. As a result, most of the farms there in the early years of the twentieth century were still a patchwork of cultivated land and sloughs, with many tufts of prairie grass and weeds marking boulders and rocky areas that had not yet been cleared.

By the end of the nineteenth century, the immigrant farmers had opened most of the new land that was available. They were ready for almost anything that would help them produce more and eliminate some of the drudgery of farm work. It was time for new machines to fill the need of ever-expanding agriculture, and inventors were busy developing the contraptions that eventually became farm tractors. The first tractors powered by internal combustion engines evolved from steam traction engines. Like the dinosaurs, some early tractors evolved into giants, which soon became extinct. Most of these early tractors were suitable only for plowing and belt work, such as threshing.

By the time my father started farming for himself, most of his farm was under cultivation, with only a few patches of prairie left in the spots that were still too wet to farm. He bought a used tractor, thinking it would take care of the slow hard job of plowing. He got it cheap enough but, unfortunately, it proved not be a bargain at any price. It was a 3-wheel Bull, a strange-looking contraption with one drive wheel on the right side, one front wheel on the right side in line with the drive wheel, and a small wheel on the left rear, called the "land wheel," using the name associated with the corresponding wheel on a plow. The land wheel did not drive or steer, it simply held up the left side of the tractor. The logic of the design depended entirely on the idea that the tractor would never be used for anything except pulling a plow. However, the design was faulty even for plowing because the plow was hitched well to the left of the drive wheel, tending to make the outfit turn to the left and putting a sideways load on the front wheel, which ran in the furrow. At best, it required a lot of room to make a right turn and was practically impossible to turn to the right in plowed ground or mud. The two-cylinder engine was temperamental, hard to start, and too small for any heavy belt work. I understand the Bull was built in two sizes, the Little Bull, and the Big Bull. Dad bought a Big Bull, but I do not know the year it was built. The one part of the rig that was successful was the plow--a two bottom Grand Detour.

After fighting the problems with the Bull tractor for a few years, Dad gave up, and went back to plowing with horses. The Bull stood in the yard for a while before he hitched a team of horses to it and pulled it into a shed. Sometime later, Mike Stripling, a neighbor who was a good mechanic, bought it for junk price and after a bit of tinkering, got it started and drove it to his place. Mike eventually dissembled the Bull and sold the parts for scrap iron. Dad went through most of the twenties and The Depression years farming with horses and did not buy another tractor until 1937. His experience with the Bull tractor was so bad that he wanted to wait until tractors were more reliable and versatile, and twenty years passed before he had enough money to buy a new one.

Evolutionary dead ends such as the Bull tractor were common in the years from about 1905 to 1920. It was said of many tractors of this era that the tractor made the farmer happy twice--*once when he bought it, and once when he got rid of it.*

Steam power was popular for threshing in the early years of the century. By the time I was born in 1927, the era of steam traction engines had come and gone. There were several steam threshing rigs in the area at one time, but by the late twenties most of them had switched to tractor power.

Julius Stripling owned the first tractor that threshed on our farm, a 40-80 Avery, running a Yellow Fellow separator by means of a long belt. He threshed all the grain in the neighborhood with the huge, heavy tractor, which was powered by a four-cylinder engine.

In those days, manufacturers of traction engines designated their models by horsepower rating. Therefore, the name meant that the 40-80 tractor developed forty horsepower at the drawbar and eighty horsepower on the belt. The 40-80 and the big separator were retired when I was a small boy. The only steam engines still in use in the vicinity when I was old enough to pay attention to such things, were Herman Warmbiers Case and Blumer Brother's Nichols and Shepard. I never learned the horsepower rating of these engines. One of my memories from the early thirties, possibly as late as 1934, was of those two engines hitched in tandem, moving a house from LuVerne to the farm across the road from our place.

The replacement of horses for all farm jobs was possible only after the introduction of tractors that could successfully plant, cultivate, and harvest crops that are planted in rows, such as corn.

Originally, all tractors had steel wheels with lugs to give them traction. While rubber tires had been tried experimentally since about 1929, no production model equipped with rubber tires on the drive wheels was tested in the Nebraska trials until 1934. However, the transition to rubber was not complete until after World War II. The war, with its accompanying rubber shortage, was a big factor in this. During the late thirties and 40's, new rims for conversion to rubber tires were in demand. Welding shops all over the country cut off the spokes of the old steel wheels, discarded the original rims and lugs, and welded the new rubber tire rims in their place. The converted wheels are now known as "cutoffs." So complete was this transition that most of the surviving tractors from that era now have cutoffs.

The Allis-Chalmers WC that Dad bought new in the fall of 1937 was a wonderful machine in my eyes. I could hardly wait until I could get a chance to drive it. It pulled a two-bottom plow, which was the same size as the horse drawn plow that required six horses. It was originally equipped with rubber tires in front and steel wheels on the rear. After World War II, we converted the rear wheels to rubber tires. From the day the WC was delivered, the horses on our farm were retired from the job of plowing forever. Transition of other farm jobs from horse power to tractor power was more gradual. All our neighbors had row crop tractors by that time.

Drawbar work for tractors, except for plowing, was constrained at first by a limited supply of implements and machinery designed to be pulled by a tractor rather than horses. Farmers simply could not afford to buy a whole new line of equipment all at once, so they built their own tractor hitches, or relied on the help of the local blacksmith to put together an arrangement to hitch the horse-drawn implement to the tractor. In fact, most equipment manufacturers reconfigured some of their earlier horse-drawn designs and marketed the products as tractor implements. The new factory-built machines were not likely to be much better than the locally built conversions. Nobody seemed to let this situation interfere with finding uses for the tractor.

Of course, I had been driving the tractor for years before I was allowed to drive the car. One of the prerequisites for being allowed to drive the tractor was being able to start it. It did not have an electric starter. While all tractors of that time had to be cranked by hand, cars had been equipped with starters for many years before that. I have often wondered why the major tractor manufacturers did not start building engines with provision for adding a starter before 1939, but that's the way it was. The major manufacturers who built their own engines did not offer electric starters until 1939. Probably, it was simply a matter of cost.

Any man, woman, boy or girl could do much more work with the tractor than with horses. Sometimes it was easier, too, but not always. Driving a 1930's vintage tractor could be hard work. Mufflers were not even an option in the original design of most tractors. The only exception, the John Deere, and the barking of its two-cylinder engine, was enough to set your ears to ringing by the end of the day--even though the muffler was standard equipment. The open exhaust of the four-cylinder tractors was worse. The noise was certain to damage the hearing of the operator who had to listen to it for long periods of time. Seats were made of steel, unpadded, and mounted on a stiff spring. Although supposedly contoured to fit the driver's bottom, they were unmerciful after a few hours of rough riding. Of course, there was nothing to dampen the vibration transmitted to the seat.

Speaking of rough riding, the steel wheels did not do a thing for operator comfort either. Power steering was still far in the future. I can still vividly recall the pain in my back from wrestling the steering wheel for hours on end. The steering wheel not only turned hard, but it also constantly fought the operator, pulling and jerking with a force that demanded a tight grip and real muscle to keep it under control. Some of the other controls required muscle as well. The clutches and brakes on these brutes were not for sissies. It may seem odd that a machine that moved as slowly as a farm tractor would need brakes.

The brakes, which were applied separately to the rear wheels, were an indispensable aid to steering. Turning, especially when pulling a load, required applying the brake hard to the rear wheel that was on the inside of the turn. Hydraulic power had not yet come to the farm, and unless the tractor was equipped with a mechanical power lift, forcing a cultivator into the ground, and lifting it out again was a weight-lifting exercise that had to be repeated hundreds of times a day.

Along with the newfound freedom and extra time that the tractor gave to farm families, there was a new element of danger. Tractor accidents happened relatively seldom, but quite often they were fatal. The Fordson, one of the early mass-produced tractors, was a particularly dangerous machine because of its nasty habit of rearing up and falling over backwards. The operator was not always the victim, either. Every now and then a small child died under the wheels of a tractor. Some power-operated farm machines seemed always ready to reach out and grab the person who became too familiar and came too close to the machinery. The corn picker was the worst in this respect. Sometimes the result was only the loss of a finger or two, but too often people were horribly mangled and sometimes killed by getting tangled in a power takeoff, the rollers, or gathering chains of a corn picker. Even the relatively slow-moving mechanism of a grain elevator claimed its share of victims. I nearly lost a thumb by getting a glove tangled in the drive shaft of an elevator. I'll write more on that later, but luckily the glove tore and peeled from my hand before any bones were broken.

Tractor farming, even considering its bad aspects, was emancipation from drudgery for farm families. Farming was still hard work, but many tasks that took months with horses could be finished in days, or a week or two, with tractor power. The weather, still the biggest risk the farmer faced, was still an uncontrollable factor, but now the chances of getting crucial jobs such as planting or harvesting done while the weather was good were much better. The chances of getting a good yield were increased because field operations could be done of the proper time. The tractor made it possible to use combines and corn pickers to eliminate most of the handwork of harvesting. The cost of operating the tractor, while it was significant, still compared favorably with the cost of supporting horses 365 days a year.

For those of us who were on the farm at the time, the tractor was a morale booster because tasks could be accomplished quicker and many jobs could be mechanized, leaving more time for other things. Considering all these factors, it is no wonder that those of us who went through this transition period still like to reminisce and admire those old clunkers whenever we get a chance.

12

Haying and Harvest

For a kid growing up on a Midwest farm in the 1930's haying and harvest were some of the most important and memorable times of the year. There wasn't just one harvest time each year. The first harvest of the year was when we cut the hay and hauled it into the barn. While gathering the hay is not what we think of when we use the word 'harvest' it was certainly an important part of the year's work. All the hay was used on the farm to carry the horses and cattle through the late fall, winter, and early spring months when pasture was not available. In the climate of northern Iowa, it was always possible to get two cuttings of hay per year and sometimes there was a third cutting of alfalfa as well. The hay fields were typically seeded with a mixture of grasses and legumes, such as timothy (a grass), red clover, and alfalfa (both legumes). Pure grass hay was better for horses, but cattle did better with clover and alfalfa. The yield per acre of grasses when planted alone was a good deal less than clover or alfalfa, so the choice of crops was a compromise aimed at achieving the best yield per acre and producing a quality of hay that was suitable for both cattle and horses.

Haying was hard work, and it had to be done in the hottest times of the year, mostly June and July. The weather was a critical factor. The period when the hay was in the best stage to be cut was short, only a few days. Frequently, it was not possible to hit this ideal stage because of rainy weather and the pressure of other farm work such as cultivation, which also had to be done within a short time frame if it was to be done at all. In any case, we would cut the hay at the first opportunity after it was ready. Rain was always a risk, but if it was not raining and there appeared to be a chance of having enough dry weather to get the job done, one of us would hitch the horses to the mower and start cutting.

I didn't like mowing. The mower vibrated violently, and the iron seat, that was uncomfortable at best, shook constantly. The driver had to sit down in fixed position with his feet braced; so there was no possibility of standing or even changing position. Believe me, it was painful after a few hours when the shaking of the seat rubbed your bottom almost raw.

Usually, the hay was left in the swath overnight. By that time, it was wilted but not dry. Raked into windrows the next day, it had to be allowed to dry completely before it was safe to put in the barn. At best, that usually took another day. If rain fell it would take longer. The quality went down with every rain, too.

In the 30's, we always put-up loose hay. Balers that could pick up and bale the hay in the field were not common until the late 30's and were scarce during World War II, so we did not bale any hay until well after the war. We usually used a hayloader which was hitched behind the hayrack and picked up the hay and elevated it into the rack. The horses and the hayrack had to straddle the windrow to do this. Dad had taught me how to hold the reins before I had to drive the team in the field, but when I was five, I started driving the horses picking up the hay. Someone was always on the rack stacking the hay as the loader delivered it, of course. Loading hay was hard work, but at least you were out in the field where there was a possibility of a little breeze, so the heat wasn't as bad as when you had to stack it in the barn.

We used slings to package the hay to lift it into the barn. A sling was an arrangement of ropes that we laid down on the rack and then stacked hay evenly on top of it. We usually used three slings to make a full load, so the load consisted of three layers of hay, each of which was picked up and hoisted into the barn separately. When we reached the barn with a load and parked it under the peak at the end of the barn, the first step was to unhitch the horses from the wagon and hitch them to the hoisting rope. The rope at this step hung in a loop from the carrier. It was a device that rolled on a track suspended from the rafters of the barn reaching the whole length of the barn and out under the peak of the roof so that the outer end was directly over the hayrack. The carrier automatically locked in place when it was pulled to the outer end of the track. The rope was always threaded through a pair of pulleys which then could be pulled down to form the hoisting loop. The next step was to hook a pulley to each end of the sling and hook a trip rope to the latch that would open the sling.

As the horses pulled the rope, it picked up the ends of the sling and rolled the hay into a tight bundle as the ends lifted and pulled together. A hard pull by the team lifted the bundle until it was in front of the big door. When the pulleys hit the carrier, it automatically locked the bundle to the carrier so it would not fall, and unlocked the carrier from its position at the end of the track. The carrier was then free to roll into the barn. It rolled fast, so the horses had to be stopped as soon as the carrier unlocked. A hard yank on the trip rope opened the sling, and the hay fell in a layer just as it had been stacked on the rack. The stacker then had to move most of the hay again with a pitchfork to fill the full width of the haymow evenly. This was hard work. The hay was heavy and hard to pull apart. The barn was almost always hot. The heat, the lack of air movement, and the chaff made stacking in the barn a tough job. Whoever was driving the team had to pull the heavy hoisting rope back by hand to make it possible to pull the carrier, using the trip rope, back to the front of the track, lock it in place, and pull the loop down so that the sling could be unhooked from the pulleys. Everything was now ready to repeat the operation. We were always glad when haying was done, not only because it was a hard job, but also because we knew we would have something to feed the livestock.

At the time I am describing, all oats, corn and soybean harvesting depended on using tractors to some extent. Before tractors evolved into machines that could completely replace horses and do every kind of farm work, they were primarily used for plowing and belt work. Every tractor had a belt pulley, and the long flat belt was the only means of transmitting power to a machine. Early in the 20th century steam engines were the popular choice for belt work, but internal combustion engines mostly replaced them by the time I was born. Dad bought the Allis-Chalmers WC in 1937 and it was our only tractor until 1946. It was a great tractor for many of the farm jobs but was too small for the heavy belt work like threshing and shelling. It did have a power takeoff that was necessary to drive the machines that came later, such as our first combine and the corn picker.

We harvested the oats in late summer, usually beginning in July and finishing in August. This was another hot job. When the oats were ripe, they were cut with a binder. Four horses pulled this machine, which cut an eight-foot swath. As it cut, it gathered the grain into bundles and tied the bundles with twine. As the binder tied the bundles it accumulated them in a carrier which could carry enough bundles to make a shock. The driver of the binder tripped the carrier when it was full leaving the bundles in bunches on the ground. The next operation was to pick up the bundles and build shocks. Shocking was entirely hand labor. Making one shock didn't amount to much, but when it was multiplied by hundreds or thousands that were required, it became a big job. A shock consisted of three or four pairs of bundles set upright with the butts on the ground and firmly braced against each other. Another bundle was set flat on the top of the shock to make a cap to help shed water. A properly built shock would withstand storms without tipping over. The shocks could stand until the grain was thoroughly dry. Even if rain fell, as it usually did before the threshing machine arrived, the shocks would quickly dry out and the grain would stay in good condition.

Threshing (always pronounced thrashing in northern Iowa) was a community affair. Probably more has been written about this part of the harvest than any other task. I think that the way we did it was quite typical in our part of the country. A neighbor owned the Avery threshing machine (properly called a separator). He used his 15-30 McCormick-Deering tractor on the belt for power. The run consisting of six farms, was probably the smallest feasible size. The machine required at least seven bundle racks to keep it running steadily. A couple of the larger farms supplied two racks, and every farm supplied at least one. Depending on the distance of the haul, more racks might be required. The bundle haulers could not set their own pace; rather the machine set the pace, and the men and teams had to keep up. The only easy part of the job was the haul to and from the field. The hardest part was pitching the bundles off the rack into the feeder of the separator because there was no chance to take even a moment's rest. Often the machine would be positioned where there was no breeze so it could be a very hot job as well. The horses had to be driven very close to the machine and stand there while the load was pitched off. It was no place to have nervous horses. At least two teams and wagons were required to haul the grain away from the machine. The grain wagons had to be backed precisely into position, and it was a big help if the team was good at backing, and the driver had to be somewhat skillful as well. Threshing time was very exciting for a little boy. From the time I was very small I was expected to help. My first job was to pick peas and beans from the garden and dig new potatoes for the meals. Of course, hauling baskets of corncobs to feed the fire was necessary too. As I got a little older, I graduated to tending the grain wagons so that they were loaded evenly and filled to capacity. That was an easy task, which could be done mostly by only swinging the grain auger to the proper positions, although a little work with a scoop shovel was required as well. The grain was weighed automatically, half a bushel at a time, before the auger delivered it to the wagon. The automatic scale that weighed the grain also included a counter. This tally was used to bill the farmer for grain threshed. Stacking the straw as it was blown out of the machine was a terribly dirty job. Dad always did that when we were threshing at our place. It made the job easier for him if someone stood on top of the machine and controlled the blower hood which directed the blast of straw and chaff, so I did a lot of that too. The blower pipe was usually set to automatically swing back and forth in an arc to spread the straw as much as possible. We needed the straw for bedding for the livestock, and unless it was properly stacked much of it would be wasted.

Feeding the crew of thirty men or so was a big job for the women. I have already mentioned my little part in it. Of course, we kids got to eat too and that was a big part of the fun of thrashing. The meals were huge and invariably displayed the cooking talents of the woman of the house. Most of them were very good cooks and well acquainted with the techniques of "feeding thrashers." Preparing extra-large meals and serving them on time without any delays required a lot of organizational skills as well as experience. There was no such thing as a schedule that could be prepared far in advance. Rain delays and even humidity in the atmosphere made it impossible to predict exactly when one farm would be finished and the rig move to the next farm. However, we always knew which farm was next in line and approximately how long it would take so it was easy enough to make a guess and then keep adjusting the estimated time forward or back as conditions permitted. It usually took a day and a half to do our farm.

The process of harvesting oats changed completely while I was growing up. The threshing runs disintegrated during the years of World War II because of the labor shortage. The threshing machine was completely replaced by the combine. Combines had been in use farther west in the wheat growing areas for several years, but the machines built for the big fields of wheat were too big for Midwest farms. The depression was also a big factor in slowing the adoption of new machinery because farmers simply could not afford to upgrade. The first small combine appeared in our neighborhood about 1938.

The widespread planting of soybeans accelerated the change to combines. Up until the late 30's beans were a minor crop, mostly grown on a small scale. While the old threshing machine was quite capable of threshing beans, there was no way to cut the plants and bring them to the threshing machine without shattering the pods and wasting a lot of the beans. Of course, the combined harvester-thresher (combine) solved that problem. Simultaneously, the production of oats went into a decline as tractors replaced horses. Unfortunately, almost no new farm machinery was built during the war. Up until 1943, we depended on neighbors who had bought combines before the war to harvest our beans. From a strictly monetary standpoint, depending on such custom operations might seem to make sense. From a practical standpoint, it was not satisfactory because of the relatively short time available to harvest the beans.

By 1943 the threshing run had gone out of existence, so it became almost imperative to buy a combine, but the only combines available for sale were well used if not worn out. Dad finally located a little John Deere 11-A in eastern Iowa and bought it. It was rusty, badly worn, and smaller than what we needed. He had the worst parts replaced but when we put it to work, we found ourselves fixing it every day. After a season or two, most of the moving parts had been replaced but it still took a good mechanic to keep it going. I spent a lot of time operating and fixing that combine and was very glad when we could replace it in 1947.

We used one piece of our old machinery for a while to harvest oats after we got the combine. In our climate it was unusual to be able to allow oats to dry enough to cut and combine at the same time. If you waited that long a lot of the heads would shatter, and the kernels would be lost or the whole plant would fall over and be impossible to harvest. Therefore, we used the old binder to cut the oats but simply did not tie it into bundles but rather allowed it to drop on the ground in a windrow. After a few days of drying weather, the grain would dry down to about 15% moisture and was ready to pick up with a pickup attachment on the combine. However, the windrows would take up moisture very quickly from rain or even dew. When the sun went down the heads would get too tough to thresh within a few minutes, and we always had to wait until the dew had dried off in the morning before starting. Using the combine was a dramatic laborsaving change from the old way. Two people could do the whole job from beginning to end, except for a completely new step, baling the straw with a pickup baler and hauling the bales into the barn or a stack. However, we did not have to hurry with the job of gathering the straw. A week or two more or less didn't make much difference.

The next harvest of the year was the job of combining the beans. Here again the weather was the most important factor. The beans matured late in the season and usually were not ready to cut until the weather turned cool in the fall. In most years the combining did not start until there had been a killing frost to knock the leaves off the plants and allow the stems to dry. Once the plants were dead the pods would dry quickly. However, they would also take up moisture very quickly if exposed to rain, or even dew. That made it necessary to move fast when the weather was dry, because later in the fall the cooler temperatures and cloudy weather made the job slower and more difficult, and there would be many days when it was impossible to combine at all. Generally, once the beans had dried in the field the first time, they would be dry enough to store if the weather was dry enough to combine. It was very unusual for the beans to get drier than the ideal moisture content of 14%. Early in the season if the weather was warm and dry, the beans would sometimes get dryer than that, but it was always a good idea to move fast while the weather was good because the risks involved in waiting for ideal conditions were too great. The combine had to be adjusted for prevailing conditions. Making an adjustment on those old combines was slow and difficult. Later combines were improved to allow adjustments while the machine was operating. That improvement made it possible to work in more adverse conditions, work longer days, and do a better job.

13

Corn Picking Time

Picking corn was the last harvest of the year, and by far the biggest. Through most of the 1930's all the corn on our farm was picked by hand, as was most of the corn in the neighborhood. It was a long job. It started when the corn first dried enough that it could be piled up without spoiling. The acceptable percentage of moisture had to be about 25% at that point. Corns cribs, whether permanent or temporary had to be built so that air could circulate through the corn and dry it. All corn was harvested and stored initially in the form of whole ears.

Picking corn by hand required a team of horses, a wagon, and a person to snap the ears off the stalks, husk them and throw them into the wagon. If there were many acres to be picked, more teams, wagons, and men were required. It had to be done with horses because in the field the horses guided themselves, following the cornrows. They started and stopped in response to voice commands or simply moved without commands, having learned when to pull ahead. The wagon was always equipped with a bangboard, a high extension of one side of the wagon, which deflected the ears, so they fell into the box as they were thrown toward the wagon. The picker had to work fast to snap and husk each ear with a minimum of movements and throw the ear without looking at the wagon. The team would pull ahead about ten feet at a time and wait for the picker to catch up. Gloves were a necessity, and the picker would usually wear a steel hook mounted on leather straps on one hand to help tear the husks off the ear. A pair of gloves would be completely worn out in a day or less. Husking gloves or mittens were made with two thumbs so that they could be turned over when one side was worn out and the other side could be worn through. We always hired extra men to pick corn. The best of them could pick 100 bushels in a day, but most could not do that well. Corn of that time yielded only 50 to 100 bushels to the acre at the most, so an acre a day per man was a pretty good average. Of course, I was still quite young when we picked by hand, but the best I could do was about 40 bushels in a day.

Pickers went to the field early in the morning as soon as there was enough light to see, came in at noon with their load, unloaded, ate, and went back out to work, coming in at the edge of darkness. This routine went on day after day, good weather or bad for weeks on end. Winter weather usually arrived before the job was finished. We were lucky to finish before the snow piled up in deep drifts.

The advent of mechanical corn pickers, like combines, was delayed by the depression. They were actually invented years before, were not improved enough to be widely accepted until the early 1930's, and by then hardly any farmers could afford them. Dad bought a used New Idea corn picker in 1939. It was a good machine that revolutionized the way we harvested. Suddenly one man with a tractor and a picker could pick corn as fast as three people could haul it away and unload it into a crib. The work was easier too. As far as weather was concerned, picking could proceed if the fields were not too muddy. The job was speeded up to the point where the risk of heavy snowfall was not great, although it still happened occasionally. Of course, there were days that were bitterly cold.

All farm machinery was somewhat risky to use, but the corn picker was more dangerous than most machines, and many farmers lost fingers, and a few lost arms or legs. Every now and then, someone was killed in a picker accident. In most cases clogging of the machinery triggered these accidents. Under the pressure to get the job done as quickly as possible, the operator would attempt to clear the stoppage with the machine running and get caught in moving parts. Before World War II, manufacturers did not shield many dangerous moving parts, and some could never be shielded. In the case of the corn picker there was no effective way to prevent a person from being caught in the snapping rollers and gathering chains. While relatively uncommon such an accident was always serious and often fatal. Power takeoff shafts could be shielded, but most of the serious injuries and fatalities resulted from clothing being caught in a power takeoff. The husking rollers were notorious for crushing fingers, and many farmers lost a finger or two in them. Even grain elevators could be dangerous.

I almost had a thumb torn off by a slow running unshielded elevator drive shaft. The shaft was only a few inches above the ground. I accidentally dropped a wrench, and it fell directly underneath the shaft. Without thinking, I made a grab for it. Remember the husking gloves with the extra thumb? I was wearing a pair of those cloth gloves. When I grabbed for the wrench, the wind blew the floppy extra thumb against the shaft and it caught and wrapped around the shaft. In a fraction of a second my hand was rolled backward around the shaft. Only the fact that the glove tore saved my hand. Almost before I had time to realize what was happening, the remnants of the glove were wrapped in a ball on the shaft, and I had a bruised hand and dislocated and sprained thumb. It was very painful but knowing that there wasn't much that could be done for it, I just pulled my thumb back in place, taped the thumb to the finger and kept on working. I was ashamed to have done such a dumb thing, so I didn't say much about it. I was fourteen years old when that happened, but I have never forgotten it. I am reminded every time I try to apply much pressure with my right thumb. It has never been the same since.

The cycle of harvesting corn was not complete until the corn was shelled or ground into feed. If the corn was used for cattle feed the whole ears of corn were often ground up. Cattle can digest the cobs as well as the kernels. The cobs add roughage to the diet as well as some feed value. Hogs can use only the kernels, not the cobs, so the corn needs to be shelled. Sometimes we let the hogs shell their own by just giving them the whole ears. They were very good at eating the kernels and discarding the cobs. Otherwise, we shelled the corn first before feeding it. Much of the corn fed to cattle was shelled, too. Horses were not allowed to eat much corn.

All corn that was not fed on the farm was shelled before being sold. The sheller was too large a machine and required too much help to operate to be practical for each farmer to own one. The owner of the sheller performed the service on demand at any time of the year. He always served a limited local area and was paid a few cents per bushel. The farmer was expected to furnish the labor to help set up for the job and feed the machine. Setting up required the assembling of sections of conveyer, called drags that rested on the ground and moved the corn from alongside or underneath the crib to the hopper of the sheller. Moving the corn into the drags required a lot of work with a scoop shovel. The farmer also had to furnish or hire two or three trucks and drivers to haul the corn to the elevator. Shelling usually took place after all the corn was picked and naturally dried out in the crib. Quite often some cribs were shelled out during the winter, but much of it was not done till the summer of the following year.

A tractor drove the older sheller rigs with a belt. The sheller required about as much power as a threshing machine. Although many of the belt driven rigs survived until shellers became obsolete, eventually there were many different setups in use, built by local welding shops. Most of them were built on trucks. Some of them used the truck engine for power. Others used a separate engine with both the engine and sheller mounted on the truck. One outfit that we hired for several years was a truck pulling a trailer-mounted sheller. The engine that drove the sheller was mounted on the truck and transmitted the power to the sheller by a driveshaft. My brother John and I helped mount the engine on the truck for that particular rig. Often the shelling business was combined with farming or trucking or both. Someone had to haul the corn to the local elevator. Trucking was a good small-town business in those days and some farmers owned trucks and hauled livestock and grain as a sideline.

Traditional paintings of harvest scenes often feature corn drying in upright piles called corn shocks. Shocking is an antiquated method of harvesting corn that disappeared in commercial corn growing areas long before I was born.

14

Silos

We did not have a silo on our farm so my only experience with filling silos came from helping neighbors. Cutting corn for ensilage started when the ears were fully filled but not dry. The stalks had to be wet as well, and the leaves were mostly still green. In my experience, the older method was to cut the corn with a corn binder, which tied the stalks into bundles. Bundle haulers immediately picked up the bundles and hauled them into where the cutter was set up next to the silo. To set up a cutter on a silo, the crew had to pull up a long pipe that connected to the blower housing of the cutter and extended up along the outside wall of the silo to the top. A curved section on the top directed the silage over the edge into the silo. Someone had to attach a pulley to the top of the silo and thread a rope through it to pull up the pipe. As a young man, I often volunteered to rig the pulley and rope. Climbing up a ladder on the outside of a silo for fifty or sixty feet and perching on the edge of the wall to do the rigging was not a popular job, and many people could not do it. The tall concrete stave silos with ladders in good condition did not bother me. I was really scared by the little old 24 or 30-foot wooden stave silos where the bolts holding the ladder were likely to be rusted out and the whole structure swayed back and forth with every step. A tractor drove the cutter by means of a belt. The haulers had to throw the heavy bundles from the racks into the feeder. The cutter chopped the entire corn plant into pieces about an inch long and blew the cut ensilage through the long pipe up to the top of the silo and over the edge. The silage then fell into the silo. Silos varied in size, but they were always cylindrical in shape, some as small as ten feet in diameter and others as much as sixteen feet or more. Height varied from 30 to 60 feet in our neighborhood. A 14 x 50' was about average. Someone had to work in the silo most of the time while filling to keep the silage leveled and distribute the heavier and lighter materials so that the filling would settle evenly.

As time passed, newer labor-saving machinery took the place of the corn binders and stationary cutters. The field chopper cut the corn and chopped it in one operation, blowing the ensilage into a wagon or truck to be hauled to the silo. At the silo, a blower blew the ensilage into the silo just as the old stationary cutter had done. Some handwork was necessary to feed the blower.

Bacterial action and fermentation in the silage starts immediately as the silo is filled and this presents a unique health hazard. The gas produced by the process is heavier than air and under certain conditions may contain a lethal concentration of a toxic component. Production of the gas starts immediately and continues for at least a couple of weeks. For that reason, it is always a good idea to run the blower for a few minutes to purge the gas before entering a partially filled silo and always leave a door open just above the level of the silage to allow the gas to drain. The gas is so deadly that one breath can kill a person. A tragedy occurred near our home community when two children climbed up and entered a silo. Both died, and when their mother went looking for them and went into the silo she died too. I also know of a case where a cow stood under the chute of a newly filled silo and died, apparently from breathing the gas draining out of the silo.

The evolution of harvesting methods has continued with the continuing development of machinery and crops. Machinery and methods of the beginning of the 21st century bear little resemblance to those of 50 to 70 years before. Tractors and combines are almost unbelievably complicated, technologically advanced, and expensive machines compared to those I operated. Of course, trucks, tractors and combines are much bigger and more powerful than they were sixty years ago. Farming is safer in many ways now than it was then, too, but it is still an inherently hazardous occupation. Modern machinery is carefully shielded whenever possible and improved design has also eliminated much of the clogging that caused operators to be exposed to dangerous mechanisms in the first place. All combines and most tractors now have cabs that make operation much safer and more comfortable. Today's farmer must be a skilled machine operator, just as the farmers of my generation were, even though we worked with relatively crude machines.

Even though I left the farm many years ago, I have remained interested it the way it is done. Farming practices have changed so much that future generations will have to rely on artifacts and stories like mine to get a glimpse of farming as it was in the first half of the 20th century.

15

Raising and Growing Our Own

We always had a large garden, about an acre in extent that took a lot of care. I was always more than willing to eat anything that came out of the garden, but I certainly did not feel the same way about taking care of it. We prepared the ground for planting with the same machinery that we used to prepare for planting corn. Planting was not hard. In fact, I enjoyed putting the seeds in the ground. The really hard work came later when the weeds came up. The weeds were always strong and healthy even if the vegetables were not. When the plants were small, the weeds were pulled by hand. To do this you had to crawl on your hands and knees, or work in a stooped position. I rebelled at this job once or twice and got a licking for it, but mostly I worked at it and dreamed of ways it could be done with a machine.

Later in the season we could do most of the weeding with a hoe, but by that time the ground was hard, so the job still wasn't easy. Potatoes were the exception to these practices, for the rows could be cultivated with a corn cultivator, and only the spaces between the hills of potatoes had to be hoed. Most of the space in the garden was devoted to potatoes, cucumbers, and melons. In our heavy black soil, plants like lettuce, radishes and carrots did well only early in the season. By midsummer, we only had to worry about peas, green beans, cabbage, and things like that. Cucumbers would usually thrive if we had a reasonable amount of rain. Squash and muskmelon would almost always produce a bumper crop. Of course, the tomatoes were always in a race with early frost. Some years we had many bushels of tomatoes, and others very few. We were not big watermelon fans, but we usually managed to grow a few. By the last part of July, we had new potatoes freshly dug from the garden for dinner and supper every day. One of the late fall jobs was to dig the main part of the potato crop. We usually had a wagonload of good potatoes, enough to last us till spring and then some. It was fortunate that we could usually count on a good crop of potatoes, for we depended on them for one of the mainstays of our diet.

Refrigeration on the farm had to wait until electric power was available, but frozen food lockers were already installed in the towns, and we made good use of them to keep meat. Butter was cooled by well water by means of a crock suspended in a cooling tank. This was a wooden tank through which the water flowed on its way from the pump to the stock tank. The major purpose for the cooling tank was to cool cream to keep it sweet until the truck from the creamery arrived to pick it up. We never sold whole milk in those days. Of course, we took all the fresh milk we wanted for our own use. Then we ran the rest of the milk through the separator. The separator was a hand-cranked centrifuge that separated the cream from the skim milk. We sold the cream and fed the skim milk to calves and pigs. Little did we imagine that in later life we would drink skim milk in preference to whole milk! We had an old wooden icebox, and sometimes an iceman delivered big cakes of ice to put in it, but for long periods of time the icebox never had any ice in it. My mother canned many quarts of vegetables and fruit each year, and we depended on those home-canned goodies. Some groceries such as flour, salt, sugar, etc. had to be purchased, but my mother always baked bread, and with that and our home-grown meat and eggs and our home-canned or fresh vegetables and our homegrown potatoes we ate very well. None of us were ever fat, but we were always well nourished.

Butchering was usually done on the farm, and although Dad could butcher a hog if he had to, I suppose, he preferred to leave the job to a professional. We usually butchered two hogs and a beef every year, although perhaps sometimes we split a beef with someone. As far back as I can remember, the meat was frozen and stored in a cold-storage locker in town, but I am sure that was a relatively new innovation and before that, meat could only be kept by canning or salting. Mother did can a little meat, but not regularly, as I recall. We ate mostly pork and beef, with a fair amount of chicken for variety, especially when we had fryers of the prime size.

Chicken for dinner meant that you had to catch the chicken first and sometimes that was quite a chase. The easy way of course was to sneak up and grab the chicken at night while it was asleep on a roost. That wasn't half as much fun as making it a fair catch in broad daylight. Then you had to chop its head off with an axe or a corn knife, wait for it to stop jumping around, scald it with boiling water, and pull off the feathers. That much of the job was exclusively for us kids to do. We then delivered the plucked chicken to the kitchen, which was entirely our mother's territory. None of us boys cooked as a general rule. I will never know whether that was really the way she wanted it, or if she just put up with it because it was the course of least resistance.

16

The Depression Years

We were all children of the Great Depression. Our parents went through a recession which was at its worst in 1921 after World War I, then experienced somewhat better times through the boom years of the twenties. From what I remember of what Dad said about it, 1928 was the last reasonably good year they had. The farmers were suffering even before the stock market crash in 1929, although of course things got a great deal worse after the crash. The prices of corn and hogs fell to their lowest level in 1932 and recovered very little until after Roosevelt instituted the New Deal in 1933. Prices really did not go up much until 1939, when the effects of World War II began to show up.

During those years we had a succession of cars, all of which were used when Dad bought them. The next one after the Model T I have already mentioned was a 1931 Model A Ford. My two older brothers, Ralph and John used it and abused it. They drove it while they were in high school and sharpened up their racecar driving skills on the gravel roads. Even though they had a few minor accidents with it, nobody ever got hurt and the car survived until it was completely worn out. The next car was a 1935 Chevy. It had a good engine but really wasn't a very good car in many other respects. It took its share of abuse too. Dad bought a new Chevy in 1940. That was the car that Phil and I learned to drive, and I must admit that it suffered from the mistakes that we made when we were novice drivers.

I have always been convinced that the depression experience changed everyone who experienced those hard times. Even children knew that there was no guarantee that life would be easy. It was inevitable that the circumstances encouraged the somewhat fatalistic belief that whatever goes up must come down, and we should be prepared when it happens. Of course, the thriftiness or penuriousness (depending on your point of view) of that generation is well known. I will have to admit that a little of that stinginess rubbed off on me, too. Everybody complained about the low prices of farm products and the scarcity of paying jobs, but they persevered in the hope that things would get better. Even most of those that were forced off the farms and had to move and find a new occupation succeeded in providing for their families somehow and eventually became more prosperous. There were casualties galore in the war against poverty, but the remarkable thing was that the survivors did as well as they did and produced the remarkably productive and optimistic generation to follow.

The people I knew did not seem to think the situation was hopeless. On the contrary, they showed a stubborn determination to make the best of a bad situation. In the short term, any job was better than no job at all, and there was always hope for better times to come.

17

Church

We attended the Evangelical church in LuVerne. My grandparents were among the families that started the congregation and built the building. In the beginning the members were predominately Swiss but a few Germans soon joined them. The people in that congregation practiced a frugal way of life and held to a rigid code of morality. The pastor who taught our catechism class was a stern and humorless old German who insisted that we memorize our lessons. My parents were always active in the church, which was not surprising since there were not many families in the church, and there was plenty of work for all.

In the Evangelical Church, the use of alcohol in any form was a sin. Even the sacrament of communion was administered with grape juice, not wine. Dancing was forbidden. Divorce was frowned upon. Smoking and use of profanity were the work of the Devil. For a long time, the congregation was unwilling to try any new music. Obviously, being a member of that church was a very serious commitment. The older members of the church strictly maintained their lifestyle in accordance with traditional teachings but found it increasingly difficult to keep their children on the straight and narrow path. Of course, the same things could be said about many churches of that time. The standards of the whole country were changing too fast for the comfort of those who grew up with traditional institutions.

The little LuVerne congregation struggled to survive throughout the depression years. The Evangelical denomination eventually merged with the United Brethren to form the Evangelical United Brethren, but that was after I had moved out of my parents' home, and I seldom attended that church anymore. Later the EUB merged with the Methodist church and the LuVerne Evangelical church building was torn down.

18

Family Living

There was a very clear division of responsibility in our household. My mother ran the house and had the last word on things concerning the household. She was a great cook and kept a clean, orderly house. She did not like anyone messing up her kitchen. Probably that was one of the reasons why I never learned to cook.

My dad ran the farm and took care of the business associated with it. He also watched every penny that came our way and accounted for all the family spending. He kept accurate, detailed records. After we moved into the new house, he had a great big roll top desk that was his personal kingdom. We were never allowed to disturb anything on Dad's desk. It belonged to the school district, but since he was the secretary and treasurer for the school board for decades, he inherited it when the school board went out of existence.

The upright piano was one of my mother's cherished possessions. She played it well enough to accompany us when singing hymns or selections from the little "Golden book." Unfortunately, she suffered from arthritis and eventually her fingers became too stiff to play. I took piano lessons from Rose Patterson in LuVerne but was never any good at it. Dad was a good singer. Families in our church would sometimes ask him to sing at funerals. He preferred to sing tenor in a duet or quartet. John, Phil, and I were all good singers. Ralph also had a good voice but for some reason, he did not participate in our family "sing-alongs." When asked, he would always decline and say that he could not sing. During our teen years, Phil and I sang in church frequently. Phil was a far better soloist than I was, so if I were offered a choice, I would always try to arrange to sing a duet with Phil. The two of us supplied our share of funeral music, too.

19

Country School

The Sherman Township Center School, pictured here as it stood in the 1990's

My brothers and I all attended the one-room country school near our farm. Officially it was designated as Sherman Township No. 5, but was also known locally as Sherman Township Center School. There are no towns in Sherman Township, so the school building located in the center of the township also served as the polling place, and the only public meeting place in the township.

The building is still in existence. The school closed in 1941, and thereafter the old schoolhouse was used only as a polling place. The windows were boarded up, and the building was only minimally maintained for over 55 years. It was the only schoolhouse of its kind still standing for many miles around, when a local group decided to preserve it and maintain it as a museum. They moved it into the town of

LuVerne and located it on the main street. Even the rocks on which it stood were moved, and the foundation was reconstructed just as it had been originally. Unfortunately, the bell is gone. Someone wrecked the little cupola that housed the bell and stole the bell, long before the preservation effort started. The roof has been repaired leaving no trace of the cupola, so the appearance of the schoolhouse is a now a little different from the way I remember it.

One teacher taught all eight grades while the school was active. I do not know the average number of students in the years before my time, but while I was in school there were usually not more than ten or twelve. The number gradually declined while I was there, dropping to five in the school year of 1940-41, when the school finally closed. I had only one classmate, Clem Stripling, when I started in the fall of 1933, and he moved away in 1935 or 1936 when I was in the third grade. From that time onward I was the only kid in my grade.

When I started school, my two oldest brothers had gone on to high school in Algona, so my brother Phil and I were the only kids in our family in the school. As I remember, the other families who were represented were Swanson, Stripling, Curran, Guy, Warmbier, Miller, Steussy and Hoversten. There may have been a Whitehill girl there too, but I am not sure about that. By the time I finished the third grade, the Hoverstens, the Striplings, the Steussys, the Whitehills and the Guys had all moved away. The Miller boys had graduated by that time as well as the Warmbiers. The Neilson family moved in where Striplings had been, and the Shipley family lived for a while where Hoverstens had been.

A homeless family lived with the Currans for a little while one winter, and their daughter attended our school while they were there. The Shipleys were poor too, and those kids had a hard time in school. They had moved frequently from one farm to another and had attended several different schools. They were all behind the rest of the kids the same age in their schoolwork, and one of them was physically handicapped as well.

In addition to our family, there were four families in the neighborhood who stayed on the same farms all through that time. They were the Swanson, Warmbier, Curran and Miller families. There were other families living in the neighborhood, but they had no children in school when I was there. The area served by our school included some farms west of us, but the families living there all sent their children to the Catholic parochial school of St. Joe. I am not including them in my description of the neighborhood, because they did not have any kids in public school and had a completely different community of interest.

When it became apparent that the school was going to be forced to close, my parents decided that I should transfer to LuVerne for my eighth grade. LuVerne began providing bus service in the fall of 1940, so I was one of the first bus riders from Sherman Township when I started the eighth grade.

Rural schools of that time were certainly constrained by lack of money, but nevertheless they did a good job of education. The curriculum was limited, and many of the books in my school were quite old. I clearly remember that some of the books I used contained penciled names of former students dated in the early 1920's, and one as far back as 1916. However, reading, writing, arithmetic and grammar were heavily emphasized. The process of learning was helped a good deal by the enforced repetition. Everyone in the room could hear teaching and recitations. The environment provided a continuous review as well. Not only did the older children hear the teacher going through the instruction for all the lower grades; the younger children heard the explanations and recitation from classes of the higher grades. Without much conscious effort they absorbed a great deal of knowledge before their time to study it.

Unfortunately for us, in that school in the late 30's, that pattern of learning worked best when there was a good representation of children of all ages. In our school some grades were missing altogether, and as I mentioned before, I had no classmates. My teacher did not bother to have classes for me a lot of the time. She just gave me assignments and

I handed them in. Of course, I got a lot of tutoring from her, too, when I gave the wrong answers.

I was always an excellent reader, having learned to read before I went to school, but I was a poor student in arithmetic. I think now that my deficiency in that area was simply because I was lazy. Reading and anything else that I could absorb by just reading, such as history, was so easy that I never learned to study. Math was a little more work, so I just did only what I was forced to do, and never got interested in it. That eventually turned out to be a paradox because I have always enjoyed doing arithmetic in my head and earned my living for most of my working career as a computer programmer, analyst, and manager, all of which involved using math. There is another personal quirk involved. All my life I have gotten in trouble in math classes. I could often give the correct answer without doing the prescribed steps that were supposed to be essential to working the problem. Consequently, I could not remember the proper method. I did enjoy the so-called story problems, where the problem was explained in words.

All I remember of the teacher I had in the first grade is her name, Gertrude Norman. In the second, third and fourth grade, our teacher was Lenore Arndorfer. She was young, and a good teacher. I liked her and was disappointed when she decided to discontinue teaching in our country school and enter a convent. She became a nun, and from what I have heard, taught in Catholic schools for many years.

After that I had Mrs. Doris Kiester. I did not like her, and she probably did not like me. She was the one that often did not bother to have classes for me. She did not supervise the playground either. I think that was the time when I really stopped liking to go to school. I did not misbehave much in the classroom, but I certainly did not cooperate unless I was forced to do so. On the playground I was often involved in fights, and some of those battles were bloody. I still have a lump on my head where Bob Neilson knocked me out with a big club. As I remember, it was a piece of tree limb about five feet long and three inches in diameter. I got a bad concussion. It is a wonder I didn't have a fractured skull. Of course, I had just bloodied his nose, so he had provocation.

Mrs. Kiester sent me home for that, but I never saw a doctor about it. In those days injuries from fighting were not uncommon and did not attract a lot of attention. If you fought, you deserved to get hurt and that was all there was to it.

In the classroom, I was often bored. I literally read every book in our little library and studied the huge old unabridged dictionary for countless hours. Nobody encouraged me to study the dictionary; I simply did it because I was fascinated by words. In fact, I was disciplined for doing it every now and then, because Mrs. Kiester thought (rightly) that I should have been spending my time doing my arithmetic instead.

When I started to school in LuVerne I found that I was way behind in arithmetic. I had some trouble getting used to being with so many kids, too. It's a good thing that the school did not label every kid that did not conform to the administratively correct pattern, as they do today. If they had, I certainly would have been labeled as some sort of a problem child. I was as good as I could be in the eighth grade, but I was really a rotten kid during the first two years of high school.

It may seem inconsistent that I have so many negative things to say, and yet I say I got a good education in country school. However, I believe that I was well educated in the fundamentals and was able to adapt to everything that came later with little effort. I was deficient in my social skills to be sure, but that was not the fault of the school; it was simply a result of my environment. I have never regretted that I started my education in country school.

20

High School

I attended high school for four years in LuVerne, Iowa, from September 1941 until graduation in May 1945. Coincidentally, those were the years that the United States was involved in World War II. The war affected our lives in almost every way during those years. It was a time of change and uncertainty, and there is no doubt that the war influenced my high school experience.

My daily routine varied somewhat depending on the season of the year. In the fall and spring, there was always a lot of farm work to be done, so I was expected to get up early enough to do some chores before getting ready and walking the quarter mile to the end of our lane to get on the school bus. I never spent much time doing morning chores on school days. Often, it was just a matter of milking two cows by hand and possibly feeding the cows and calves, then coming in for breakfast, and getting ready for school.

In the winter, when fieldwork was impossible, I often did no chores at all in the morning, just got up, ate breakfast, and went to catch the bus. All through the war, we were on war time, the same as daylight saving time. As a result, it was still dark at 7:00 when left the house during most of the winter months.

The morning bus ride was usually a pleasant experience. I got on the bus about 7:10 AM and arrived at school at 8:30. Often, our farm was the first stop on the route. I always looked forward to sitting with my friends and talking during the long ride to school. I did not meet Irvin Mertz and the Casey brothers, Clarence and Eugene, until I started high school, but we soon became good friends. Clarence and I, especially, have kept in touch and remained close friends all our lives. Most of the rides were completely uneventful. There were never any disciplinary problems that I can recall. A few times the bus got stuck in a snowdrift or bogged down in mud, and once it slid off a muddy road and teetered on the edge of a deep drainage ditch. When things like that happened, there were always farmers with tractors willing to help, so the bus would be pulled out and back on the route before long. We seldom missed a day of school because of weather or bad roads.

The school day usually started with band practice. I never had any athletic ability whatsoever and did not participate in sports. I really was not very good at playing the clarinet, but I liked music and took advantage of every opportunity to play or sing. I was in the band all four years and sang with a chorus and boy's quartet. Almost all the things I enjoyed most in high school related to music in one way or another. In a way, that is amazing, because there were many others with far more talent than I had who played in the band and sang, but really didn't seem to value the experience as much as I did. This has evolved into a pattern for me. All my life I have loved to sing, and have never been particularly good at it, but I just don't want to give it up.

After band, my school day went downhill in a hurry. I don't know what the matter with me was, but during my freshman and sophomore years I was a real jerk. My class was one of the worst behaved that ever attended LuVerne High. I was as rebellious as anybody else in the class was, and worse than most. We had a very high turnover of teachers. Most of the male teachers went into the service early in the war. Several of their replacements were middle-aged women who had not taught for years, and really did not want to teach, but took over because somebody had to do it. For a while we had a succession of teachers who started quitting after only a couple of months. I am afraid our class behavior was one of the big reasons why some of them quit.

From this vantage point of more than sixty years later, I perceive that at least part of our bad behavior was a reaction to the stress of current events. Most of us had close relatives in the armed services. All of us knew people who were fighting and dying in the war. The graduating classes that preceded mine during the war years suffered terrible casualties. LuVerne was a small school, with only 90 to 100 students total during those years. Usually there were ten boys or less graduating each year. By the time I graduated, there were eight boys I had known who had been killed in the war, and three others who were wounded or prisoners of war. One of the girls in the class of 1944, Mary Barton, was a widow before she graduated. She married Bob Hoversten, who attended our country school before his family moved to the Bode area. Just a few months after they were married, he was killed.

My grades were not particularly good during the first couple of years. In most of my classes I did not do anything I wasn't forced to do and did not like school. The only exceptions were band and our shop class, which was called manual training in those days. Of course, I learned some things despite my attitude, but I know I could have done much better. The junior year was better, but it was not until my senior year that I finally got into a class I really enjoyed. It was, of all things, bookkeeping. I discovered that I really liked working with numbers, if they concerned something important such as money. Having grown up during the Depression, I was very conscious of the necessity of having money, because we saw very little of it during my childhood.

One of our favorite forms of recreation during those years was shooting. Phil and I bought a .22 rifle, and somewhere along the line we acquired a 12-gauge shotgun, too. We burned up box after box of .22 shells, but the shotgun shells were too expensive to waste, so we reserved them mostly for hunting. On the other hand, we could afford to shoot at anything we wanted with the .22. Mostly though, we did target shooting.

During the war years, many things were rationed. The most important of these to me were gasoline and tires. On the farm we always had enough ration stamps for tractor gas to do the farm work, although we still used horses a great deal. I am sure my dad considered the availability of tractor gas in choosing which jobs to do with the tractor, when there was a choice between using the tractor or horses. Car gas was rationed much more strictly. We had to restrict our use of the car to necessary trips to avoid running out of stamps before the end of the month. That restriction meant that we boys had to choose our school activities very carefully, because we were allowed very few extra trips to town to attend school functions, and our only option for daily transportation to and from school was the school bus. Even travel between schools via the school bus was a rare occurrence, something that was not done much more than once a year.

Tires were a big problem. The tires on our car wore out early in the war. After that only used or retreaded tires were available. We often wore out the tread on those tires. They almost always blew out before the tread rubber was worn off. Blowouts occurred so often that we considered them routine annoyances. Even before I started driving, I became an expert at changing tires. By the time that new tires became available again after the war, I had experienced blowouts on almost every conceivable type of road surface, and during all kinds of weather. I could change a tire on our 1940 Chevy in seven minutes, even on the shoulder of a wet gravel road.

I did not get my driver's license until I was 17. Of course, I had been driving the tractor long before that and by the time I was 14, I was expected to work a full day driving the tractor and do anything a grown man would do with it. I drove the car around the farm, too, but my parents would never let me drive on the road until I got my license. Just two years after I finally got a license to drive the car, I got a chauffeur's license, which entitled me to drive a truck. In those days an Iowa chauffeur's license was unrestricted, except for driving a bus. One license was all that was required to drive a truck of any size or configuration.

I was always fascinated by machinery, and I learned a great deal about building and using tools and machinery during those years, mostly at home on the farm. I did not like the job of mowing the lawn, so by the time I was a sophomore in high school I had built my first power lawn mower. I built three of them while I was in high school, and they all worked. Not only did I use my mowers to mow the lawn at home; but also got a part time job mowing the LuVerne cemetery. My machine was the first power mower ever used there. It was probably the only one in the area at the time. I also tried my hand at designing other devices, but never built them. For example, many years later I ran across a design for a front-end loader that I had drawn while I was still in school but did not have the resources to build. It was a good practical design, very much like some that were successfully manufactured and marketed a few years later. I had worked out the angles of force and working loads on key parts of the mechanism, too. At the time I rediscovered the drawings, our son Dave was a student at Colorado School of Mines working on his engineering degree. He checked my figures and found that they were quite accurate. The ironic part of this story is that when I was in school, I almost flunked geometry, but during the same period was able to apply a good working knowledge of geometry. Obviously, I understood what it was all about despite my dismal grades in the classroom.

Transcript of High School Credits

THIS CERTIFIES THAT James Archer Blumer

Address Livermore (City or Town) (Street No. or R. F. D.) Iowa (State)

was a student in the Luverne High School for 8 Semesters from Sept 1 1941

to May 16 1945 He was graduated in May 1945 Below is a complete record of the work of this student in this High School. Credits recorded in red ink were earned in other schools, namely: (Name of H. S.) (State)

YEAR	SUBJECT	No. Wks.	Recitations per Wk.	Length of Rec. in Min.	Lab. Per. per Wk.	Length of Lab. Per. in Min.	Mark	Unit of Credit Earned	REMARKS
1	Algebra	36	5	60			C+C	1	
1	English I	36	5	60			B+B	1	
1	General Science	36	3	60	2	60	A+A	1	
1	Industrial Arts I	36			5	60	B+C	1	
2	Geometry	36	5	60			C+D	1	Number in class 80
2	English II	36	5	60			B+B	1	Rank in class 4
2	World History	36	5	60			B+A	1	
2	Biology	36	5	60			B+A	1	
3	American Literature	36	5	60			A+A	1	
3	American History	36	5	60			B+B	1	
3	Typing I	36			5	60	D+F	½	
3	Sociology	18	5	60			A	½	
3	Economics	18	5	60			A	½	
4	English Literature	18	5	60			A	½	
4	Physics	36	3	60	2	60	B+A	1	
4	Industrial Arts II	18			5	60	A	½	
4	Government	18	5	60			A	½	
4	Algebra II	18	5	60			C	½	
4	Speech	18	5	60			A	½	
4	Vocations	18	5	60			B	½	
4	Bookkeeping	18			5	60	B	½	
					Total Units			16	

I Certify that the foregoing is a correct transcript for the student named.

Signed (Prin.) (Supt.)

Address

Date

SYSTEM OF MARKING USED IN THIS SCHOOL

A, to indicates Superior
B, to indicates Above average
C, to indicates Average
D, to indicates below average
F, to indicates Failure

My High School Report Card

21

Girls

And then there was the matter of girls. I was interested in girls and I liked them, but I didn't have any idea how to deal with them. The fact that I grew up in a household of boys didn't help matters either. I suppose that in the social realm I was not much different than most of my peers. Most of us did not start dating at all until we were about 17, and then it was rather tentative for quite a while. All my social experiences with girls were in group activities until my senior year. I never had a real date while I was in high school.

The first girl I ever kissed was Erna Eustace. She was a nice girl, smart and pretty. I liked her, and I guess she liked me too, but I was far from being ready for anything more than that. She got married within a year after we graduated to a guy from Ft. Dodge, and that marriage has lasted a lifetime.

There were ten girls in my class, some good friends but others just friendly acquaintances. Most of the girls in the class married soon after graduation. The majority married within a year or two, and a lot of those marriages ended in divorce. Dale Brayton and Ruth Ann Gronbach were sweethearts in high school and married soon afterward. They were the only classmates who married within the class. That was a lifetime marriage, too. I spent a lot of time in my teen-age years thinking about girls but never did much about starting a romantic relationship. As inept as I was in social skills, it is probably just as well that I didn't.

I worked a little harder towards the end of my high school years than I did at the beginning, but I never worked very hard. I never really learned how to study. My parents considered academic achievement to be important, which was to be expected since they had both been teachers. While I agreed with that idea, I was an under-achiever. I have never been competitive by nature. I have always been willing, or even happy, to let others take the top honors. I finished my high school years in fourth place in the class. The three who ranked above me were some of my best friends. My friend Grace Christensen was valedictorian, Irvin Mertz was second, and Erna Eustace was third. Grace has always told me I should have been first. Whether that is right or not, it is ancient history now, and probably had no effect on what we have done with our lives in the half century that has passed since then.

22

Between The Wars

After I graduated from high school, I spent the next year working on the farm. I had been doing a great deal of the farm work while I was still in school because all my brothers were in the armed services. Ralph and John were both in the Army Air Corps (the predecessor of the Air Force). Ralph was in what was called the China Burma India Theater. He spent most of the war in India and China as a crew chief on a B-29, moving to Tinian Island in the Pacific towards the end of the war. John was in Italy, flying a P-38 fighter. Phil was in the Army, still in the U. S. at the end of the war, although he was one of the first occupation troops to go into Japan after the war ended. That left Dad and me to run the farm, and it was a lot of work. I was drafted in December 1945 and went for my physical but was deferred because I was needed on the farm. The war veterans were coming home in droves by that time, and the Army did not need me anyway. I did not have much of a chance to do anything except stay home and work until after John came home in 1946. Ralph and Phil never came back to live at home after the war, but they occasionally came for short visits.

Until John returned and started taking over the farm, I did not really spend much time thinking about what I wanted to do. I had a full-time job, and I liked it, although Dad didn't pay me very much in addition to my room, board, and the use of the family car. However, that was sufficient for that stage of my life. I saved most of the wages I earned from working on the home farm. From time to time, I took temporary jobs when I was not needed at home, mostly working on other farms or as a laborer in construction. I loved working on machinery and began acquiring tools as they became available. I spent virtually everything I made at my incidental jobs in the tool departments of Sears and Montgomery Ward. During the war there simply had been no tools to buy, and I felt like a kid in a candy store when they began appearing in the stores again. I still have some of those tools after using them all my life. My big purchase at that time was a welder. I taught myself how to weld and used that machine for most of the rest of my life. In fact, I finally sold it in 1999, after having owned it for 52 years. We built a shop on the farm, and that became the place where you could find me almost any time if I wasn't working somewhere else.

23

College and Radio Days

By 1947, I was getting restless, and felt that I really should be getting away from home. I decided to go to college. It wasn't that I had any real desire to go to school again; it just seemed like the thing to do. Phil was out of the Army by that time and going to Luther College on the GI bill. I had no desire to go into the armed services. As a matter of fact, the Army, Navy and Air Force were downsizing, not drafting or encouraging enlistment at that time. Obviously, I made the decision to go to college for the wrong reasons, but I was not mature enough to realize that at the time.

At Luther College, I shared a room with Phil in a house off campus. Very little housing was available on campus at that time. Most of the single veterans lived in old surplus Army barracks that had been moved to the campus after the war. The college used some other war surplus buildings as classrooms. While most of the guys in my freshman class were recent high school graduates, the veterans far outnumbered the male postwar high school graduates in the sophomore, junior and senior classes. I felt that I fell in between the predominate groups in many respects because I had very little in common with the kids who graduated from high school in 1947. I felt much more comfortable with the older guys. Most of the girls, of course, were fresh out of high school.

Yours Truly

I had to get a job immediately, because I was not getting any more money from home, and I spent most of my savings for tuition, books and room and board. Within a few days after I arrived in Decorah, I got a job working in a gas station. While the job certainly was not hard, it took all the evening hours that I should have used for studying; furthermore, it completely shut out my social activities. I was not happy with the arrangement and soon started looking for something else.

Within a couple of weeks after school started, I saw a notice that a part-time job was available in the college radio station, KWLC. I interviewed and got the job. The morning hours suited me much better. I worked a two-hour shift from 7:00 to 9:00 A.M. three days a week, and 9:30 to 11:00 A.M. two other days. I gave the gas station owner two weeks notice and quit after having worked there only a month. I loved working in the radio station. I learned far more there than I did in any class. I only worked in the control room. I never did any broadcast work at the college.

At the end of the first semester a job opened at the commercial radio station in Decorah, KDEC, and I took it in addition to the other job. For that one, I had to get up early to be at work at 5:30 AM every weekday.

The station went on the air at 5:30, and I took on more responsibility I soon found that I needed to get there even earlier. On the days I worked the early shift at KWLC I had no time to waste between jobs. I left the downtown studios at 6:30 and rushed back to the campus to start there at 7:00. Luckily, there was very little traffic at that time of day. I had bought an old car, but when the weather was good enough, I rode a bike back and forth. It was only three or four miles. I didn't even own the bike. One of my friends owned it, but he hardly ever rode it and was willing to let me use it.

My first early morning chore at KDEC was to turn on the lights, turn on the proper switches on the control console, make sure the microphones were in the proper places, and check the mics. Of course, an engineer had to be on duty at the transmitter that was located some distance from the studio. After the first few days, the management entrusted me with the job of turning on the link to the transmitter and playing a recorded announcement that started the broadcast day. All recordings were on big platters then. I do not know if the tape recorder had been invented yet. I do know that I had never heard of one at that time. We had the primitive ancestor of the tape recorder, the wire recorder, but the sound quality of a wire recording was so bad we seldom played one on the air. Before I had been there very long, I started preparing the first news broadcast of the day. It was supposed to be the announcer's job, but he hated to get up early, and was in the habit of rushing at the last possible moment, completely unprepared to read the news.

Our news all came in on the Teletype. The Teletype would hammer away all night long, unattended, feeding through a roll of paper. In the morning when I came in there was a huge mess of paper in the basket behind the machine. The station manager taught me how to prepare the early news broadcast. The first step was to gather up the armload of paper from the Teletype and dump it on the floor at the end of a long table. Then, armed with a steel ruler to use in tearing the paper, I would stand beside the table, find the beginning of the roll of paper, pull it across the table and begin reading the stories. Each story had a heading, which made it easy to spot the beginning of the story.

Reading as fast as possible, I would make a quick decision as to how important the story was, tear it off, and flip it upside down on a pile. I would start as many piles as necessary, with the most important on my right and going down in importance from there. When I had separated all the stories, I would start from the left-hand side, turn each pile face up, and stack the piles into one stack in order of importance with the least important on the bottom. After completing the stack, I would carry the whole thing into the studio and place it in front of the microphone. The announcer was supposed to edit the news, but often he didn't get there in time to do more than sit down and run through a few exercises to get his voice warmed up. Precisely on time, I would turn on the mic and the "On Air" light, and he would start reading. He was pretty good at reading as though he knew what he was talking about, and probably the listeners never suspected that he had no more idea what was coming next than they did. There was always more material than he needed to fill a fifteen-minute broadcast. I did nothing with commercials except to make sure the copy was on the table. I went through this whole early morning ritual to get the station out of bed, and before most of the regular employees came in, it was time for me to leave.

At KWLC, my duties were mostly to run the console, which controlled the mics and the turntables, and to play records. We had 16 RPM, 33 1/3 RPM and 78 RPM records, and a lathe to cut new records. Cutting platters on the lathe was our only method of recording. The real benefit I got from working there, however, was the opportunity to learn how radio transmitters and receivers worked. Oliver Ettriem, the founder and chief engineer of KWLC, built the original transmitter himself, and for years maintained it with very little help. He was eager to pass on his knowledge to someone else, and frequently would explain what he was doing as he worked on the equipment. He encouraged me to read books that he had lying around and gave me a junk box so I could build circuits myself. My major project was to build an amplifier, not that anybody needed it, but just as a learning exercise. Of course, the transistor had not been invented yet so all my work was with vacuum tubes. It was a wonderful opportunity, but it came to an end all too soon.

I was not doing well in school at all, and never went back after the end of my freshman year. Chemistry was the subject that defeated me. I dropped it before the end of the year. I got lousy grades in algebra as well. It became obvious that I needed a lot of remedial work and training in how to study before I was ready for college. I had a chance to enroll in a trade school, RCA Institute in New York, and was assured that I could probably get some financial aid. I didn't take advantage of it. New York seemed as remote as the moon to me at that time, and I had no desire to go there.

I went back to the farm and fell into the same pattern as before, the only difference being that I started living and working off the farm most of the winter. I worked for a construction company in Algona for a while, a warehouse and trucking company in Waterloo, Iowa for a while, and the last winter before I went into the Army, I worked for an implement company in Algona. I had decided I wanted to farm, and I bought a new Oliver 70 tractor in the fall of 1948. I rented some land and was now a self-employed farmer.

The Korean War started in about August of 1950, and the draft mechanism that had been little used since the end of World War II went into high gear again. I got a draft notice almost immediately and got a routine deferment for three months to harvest my crop. I went for my physical exam and was inducted into the Army on January 16, 1951.

24

Army Days

My brother John, Me, Father (Paul), Brother's Ralph and Phil

I was inducted into the Army at Fort Des Moines Immediately after being sworn in. We were herded into a train headed for Fort Riley, Kansas. Fort Riley was the home of the 10th Infantry Division at that time. It was only a training division during the Korean War. Arriving at Camp Funston early in the morning, we immediately began the process of shedding our civilian identity and being turned into soldiers. Of course, it was a big adjustment, but I don't think that it was as hard for me as for a lot of others. I was used to getting up early, taking orders, and working hard.

I was never an athlete and was clumsy and uncoordinated. One of the first incidents that I remember from my basic training days, occurred when our grouchy drill sergeant first started teaching us how to march. After a few minutes, he planted himself in front of me. While I stood rigidly at attention, he delivered an oration that went something like this:

"Whenever I get a bunch of new recruits, I know none of them know how to march. Half of them don't know their left foot from their right. But so help me God, this is the first time I ever saw a recruit that is twenty-one years old and hasn't learned how to walk yet!'

He was wrong about one thing. I wasn't 21 years old; I was 23.

We went through basic training in eight cold, exhausting weeks. The only minor triumph I remember was near the end when we had to go through the obstacle course as a part of our final test. Finally, I found something that I could do well. Actually, most of the obstacles were not much different from the things I got used to when I was a kid on the farm. I was the first to finish in my group. The corporal who was of the end of the course told me I did really good and then ordered me to go through it again. As a result, I went through it twice while everybody else only had to do it once. Finally, basic was over. I was never so glad to get through anything, as I was when we got to the end of it.

Sometime during those first weeks we all had to take tests to determine if we had any aptitude for special training. The chances of drawing anything but immediate deployment or advanced infantry training were not good, because of the urgent need for infantry riflemen and other combat troops. The majority of the guys who were in basic with me went directly to FECOM, the Far East Command, which of course meant Korea. The casualty rate in Korea was horrible at that time.

We got a weekend pass at the end of basic, but got our new orders before we left, so I knew right away that I was going into specialized training in communications. I was glad to get the assignment, of course, but would probably have chosen mechanics training if I had been given a choice.

The communications school was right next-door, in Service Battery, 35th. Field Artillery Battalion. It was just starting when I was assigned there. I was in the first class and spent the first week working in the supply room, unpacking supplies, and building makeshift training aids. The class was small, only about a dozen guys and most of the training was so easy it was ridiculous. The only thing that was completely unfamiliar to me was pole climbing. However, I managed to get through it without too much trouble, although I was certainly not an expert climber by the time I finished. There was a pair of twins in the class, the Scott brothers, who had been linemen for a power company in Nebraska. They were a big help to those of us who had never put on a safety belt and hooks and climbed a pole. We also had one man who had been an installer for Western Electric, Bill O'Quinn. Our battery commander was a reserve officer who had been recalled to active service after being an installation foreman for Western Electric. There were also others who had civilian experience in communications. As a group we were well qualified for the assignment. Initially, it was not clear whether I was to get radio training or telephone training, but after receiving low marks on the Morse code aptitude test, I was assigned to the field wireman section.

The electrical theory class was a review for me because I had learned the subject well in the radio station while I was in college. Telephone and switchboard repair was also fun; because a lot of it was very similar to the work I had done on radios.

Two weeks before we were scheduled to graduate, I was ordered to report to the battery commander. I was puzzled and a little bit scared because I couldn't think of any reason why I would be in trouble, and I knew I had been doing very well in all the subjects. In the battery commander's office, the interview went something like this:

"Private Blumer, the electrical theory instructor has reported to me that you think you know more about the subject than he does."

There was only one truthful answer I could give:

"Yes, Sir."

As a matter of fact, I knew far more than the instructor did, and I often explained things in class while he listened. In military classes that doesn't happen very often, but that was one place we could get away with it.

"Well, Private, you are going to get a chance to prove it. You are assigned to teach the class to the next group of trainees, starting next week."

Technically, I never made it to the scheduled end of my training. By the time my class graduated I had already been assigned to the cadre and had been teaching for a week. However, I wasn't alone. Bill O'Quinn was teaching telephone and switchboard repair, and the Scott brothers were teaching pole climbing.

I taught the same subject for more than a year. We usually started a new class of trainees every Monday morning, and I had them for two weeks. If my memory is correct, the last class that I taught was the 46th to go through the course. I got very good ratings when my class was inspected, too. In fact, somewhere I still have an inspection report where I got the highest rating in the entire 10th Division for the month.

Of course, I learned a lot during that year too. Since the students were mostly draftees, there was a tremendous range in their qualifications. Some were illiterate for all practical purposes. At the other end of the scale, I had some college students, even some who were in their second or third year working toward an engineering degree. Those guys were National Guard men whose unit had been activated. The variety of students made the job much more interesting. Of course, the prescribed textbook was the Army training manual, which was very simple. To keep the class interesting, I quoted from Bell System practices that I learned from Bill O'Quinn, as well as a college physics textbook. Naturally, I could not let the students see those other references but kept them under wraps just to help me prepare my lectures. I designed my own training aids and built some of them myself. The fact that I had my own classroom building helped a lot. Like all the other classrooms, it was a one-story temporary building left over from World War II.

Arlene and I got married during this time. I have written about this elsewhere. I lived off post in Manhattan after I was married. I really liked what I was doing, and there was no doubt that I was in a far better situation than most GI's during that time. I was promoted to Corporal too which helped a little bit with the money. We never had much money.

My soft job came to an end in May 1952. I got my orders to go to FECOM the same day our first baby, David, was born. After a two-week leave, which we used to move Arlene and David back home to Iowa, I was on my way to Korea.

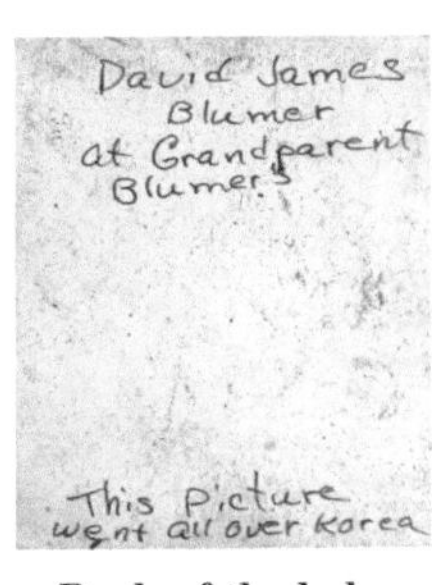

Back of the baby picture shown, reads: "David James Blumer at Grandparent Blumers, This picture went all over Korea"

After processing for three days at Camp Stoneman, near Martinez, California, I shipped out from San Francisco on the General Howze bound for Yokohama, Japan. I got another lucky break almost immediately on-board ship. Announcements on the ship's PA System asked for volunteers, and one of them specified someone with communication experience. I volunteered without knowing what I was volunteering for. It turned out to be the disc jockey job. At certain hours during the day, they played records and tidbits of news and information from the States on the PA system, and it became my job to do it. While most of the 5000 or so troops on that ship had absolutely nothing to do unless they got stuck with some dirty detail, I spent every day in a corner of the ship's radio room, planning and broadcasting.

I was smart enough to keep my mouth shut in the troop compartment, and if anybody noticed that I disappeared every day for 8 hours, they never paid any attention. I remember hearing some bitching that the same songs got played over and over, and it was true. The record library was not big enough to last two weeks without quite a bit of repetition.

At Yokohama, we went directly from the ship to a train that took us to Camp Drake. We were processed through there in less than three days and hauled back to Yokohama where we boarded the General Howze again for the trip to Pusan. The ship was not as crowded as it had been crossing the Pacific. It was hot and humid in Pusan. Disembarking there was a good deal slower than it had been in Yokohama, because while we marched directly from the ship to a train, the trains were far more primitive than the one we had ridden in Japan. It took many trains to accommodate all the troops who were on their way to North Korea.

The train we boarded was pulled by a little steam locomotive. There were four or five passenger cars and two open gondola cars, one in front just behind the tender and one at the back of the train. The seats in the cars were simply wooden planks on each side extending the length of the car forming a bench with no back other than a board on the side of the car. The glass had been removed from the windows. Most of the time that was good because it gave us ventilation, but it got very smoky when the train went through a tunnel. There were several tunnels on the route. Even when we were not in a tunnel, we sometimes got some smoke in the cars. The engine did not have enough power to move the train very fast, and when we got into the mountains our progress was very slow on the upgrades. In fact, we took turns getting off and walking beside the train on some of the long grades. It felt good to walk after sitting on those benches, and it was easy to keep up. Guards were always stationed in the open gondola cars at the front and back of the train. It took twenty-nine hours for the trip from Pusan to Kumwha, with several stops to take on coal and water, and let off some of the troops. The cars were very dirty of course, and by the time the trip was over, we were all pretty well covered with soot.

We arrived at the end of the line at Kumwha Junction in a pouring rain. Truck drivers from many different outfits were waiting, and there was some confusion until everyone found the proper truck, but in a few minutes, I found the truck I was looking for and got on. There were four of us on the truck. In the combat zone no vehicles were permitted to use the canvas cabs or the canvas covering over the truck bed, so there was no protection from the rain. Even though we wore ponchos we were soon soaked. It was not a pleasant ride. It seemed like a very long time before we arrived at C Battery, 31st Field Artillery Battalion, but it probably was not more than an hour. When we arrived at the battery motor pool and got off the truck, someone directed us to our respective sections.

I was the only replacement going to Detail Section. I remember trudging through the mud to the Detail Section squad tent. There I met my sergeant, Sal Cassaro, who assigned me a space in the tent with a cot and told me I was on my own until the next morning. The only unpacking I could do was to get my blankets and my mess kit out of my duffel bag and make the bed. I discovered that my blankets were very wet too, but there was nothing I could do about it. It was late in the day, and chow was ready, so as soon as I could, I ate and went to bed shortly after dark. All I could hope for was that the blankets would dry out from my body heat. I was exhausted and I slept, but the thunder of the 155mm howitzers firing most of the night kept waking me up. I don't remember much of anything of the first week or so after that, except that it rained most of the time, and it was almost impossible to get clothes and bedding really dry.

The outfit had been in the same location for a little while, so the living arrangements were not bad. The war in Korea by that time had settled down to a sort of artillery war period more like World War I than World War II. We always considered the enemy force to be Chinese, which probably was accurate. We did not normally see enemy soldiers, but to the best of our knowledge there were far more Chinese than North Koreans, and the Chinese were definitely in command. It was frustrating for us because it was clear that we were there to fight a holding action, not to go all-out to win the war. We were not supposed to call for fire on an enemy location unless they were shooting at us. Believe me, that did not mean that things were quiet. The Chinese artillery on the mountain shelled us from time to time across the river from our position. Sometimes we would retake some land, but more often the Chinese would push us back a mile or two.

The tent was good protection from the rain. We had Korean KP for "kitchen patrol" boys who did our laundry for us when the weather was good enough and hung the clothes out on bushes to dry. Of course, they did all the washing by hand. We appreciated the service and paid them a little in Korean money. They helped in the kitchen tent and the mess tent too. They were the only Korean civilians we ever saw in the combat zone.

We moved up a little closer to the front after I had been there two or three weeks. Since we were now in easy reach of the Chinese guns, and even mortars, there was no more living in tents. We dug holes in the ground and roofed them with sticks and sandbags to form bunkers. The only tents still in use were the kitchen, the mess tent, and a little tent for the switchboard. Actually, we often did not eat in the mess tent, because the Chinese had a nasty habit of shelling us at chow time. For some reason that usually happened in the evening, so breakfast was in the mess tent most of the time. Otherwise, we just grabbed our food and took it back to the bunker to eat.

Speaking of food, we always had enough to eat. Was it safe to eat? Usually, yes. Was it appetizing? Often it was not. Apart from things that were baked by our cooks, almost all of it came out of cans. That was not a bad thing in itself, but if you looked at the dates on the cans, you had no trouble figuring out why the stuff tasted bad. Much of what we ate was canned during World War II, some of it as far back as 1942. Ten-year-old meat is not exactly gourmet food, and weenies and beans sort of degenerate into unappetizing goo.

Living in a bunker had advantages to offset the fact that you lived in a hole with dirt walls, dirt floor, and a sandbag roof that leaked when it rained. The main advantage, of course, was that only a direct hit was likely to hurt you. The other advantage was that when the weather started to turn cold, the bunkers stayed at a fairly constant temperature. We had a little stove that helped a lot to keep things reasonably dry. Of course, rats liked the bunkers too, and we soon got used to having rodents scurrying around, especially when there were no lights in the bunker. The closest we ever came to a direct hit on the bunker was when an artillery shell exploded only ten feet from the door. I was in the bunker at the time, lying on the floor, and I got a shower of sand from the sandbags. I realized afterward that it was a wonder that the dirt wall did not cave in, but it held. One of the silly little things I remember from about that time was from another shelling. At the first explosion I hit the dirt, and while I was lying there waiting for the shelling to stop, I noticed that my head was right next to a wooden crate full of empty Coke bottles. I was thinking that it wasn't very smart to put myself so close to something that could turn into deadly shrapnel.

When we were in one place for quite a while there really was not a lot of telephone work to do. I usually made the rounds of the gun sections and the fire direction center every day to check out the phones and replace batteries if necessary. Since all the wires were lying on the ground, they got damaged frequently so I had to fix or replace them as necessary. Otherwise, most of what I did was just float around and do whatever work was necessary at the time. I dug holes, filled and stacked sandbags, and unloaded and stockpiled ammunition when a truckload arrived. Our battery truck driver often needed help loading ammo from the stockpile and unloading it at the gun emplacements. When we were doing a lot of firing, we often did not stockpile ammo at all, just unloaded it at the guns as it came in, which was at night more often than not.

Actually, the only injury I got while I was in Korea was while I was unloading ammo at night. It was a really stupid accident. It was very dark, and I thought I had unloaded all the projectiles off the truck, which was parked so that the front end was higher than the rear. I was standing at the rear of the truck leaning my butt against the tailgate. Unknown to me, there was still one projectile left on the truck. The truck was running, and apparently the vibration dislodged the 85-pound projectile, and started it rolling to the rear of the box. It struck me in the small of my back and knocked me flat on the ground. Luckily, it fell clear of my legs, or it undoubtedly would have broken my leg. I got a painful bruise, but that was the extent of my injury. I never reported it.

Charlie Herchenhan was our driver for the detail section, and he took care of most of our transportation needs with a 3/4-ton weapons carrier. Occasionally, we could get another weapons carrier from the motor pool, and I drove it whenever I could get a chance. Usually that was for routine details such as going down to the river to fill sandbags, but when we moved, I usually hauled a load of telephone wire and odds and ends. A lot of my activity was simply housekeeping, such as helping build the frames to support the cots so that we could double deck them in the bunker. We made those frames out of sticks tied together with telephone wire. It seemed as though whenever we were getting close to getting everything fixed up so that we could live fairly comfortably, we moved and had to start over again.

About that time, I had my first bout with an unidentified illness. It hit me early one morning when I was on guard duty just before dawn. I don't remember feeling bad when I first got up and went out to walk my guard detail, but then I suddenly got a very bad headache, and the next thing I knew I was lying face down in the mud. I developed a high fever and felt awful for a couple of days, but never left the outfit. I lost some weight too. I went on sick call but did not get any treatment other than the usual aspirin and was never off duty.

In the fall, some of us went on an exercise called a turkey shoot. The name came from an American pioneer sport where a live turkey was tethered behind a log, and the competitors shot at it from a position where they could see only the turkey's head when he raised it up. The analogy to our tactics is that we were playing the part of the marksmen, shooting at targets that were usually concealed, or out of range of our guns. Those of us who went on that turkey shoot were very lucky to come back rather than be captured or killed.

I wrote the following story of the turkey shoot about twenty years ago, and I am including it just as I wrote it when the memory was still fresh.

Back of the picture on the left, reads: "Taken at the bunker up on Turkey Shoot, The old Position, Chorwon"

For the record, I would like to tell about an experience in Korea that I have seldom mentioned, partly because it brought back too many bad memories, and partly because nobody would believe it anyway. At the time, our battery was in the hills on the south side of a river, the name of which I can't recall. It is a fairly big river, with a flood plain a mile wide. We had a line of tanks and infantry outposts on the north side of the river, but most of our forces were on the south side. I got volunteered as a member of a special eleven-man detail equipped with two 155mm howitzers, the artillery tractors which pulled them, two ammunition trucks, a jeep and the 3/4-ton weapons carrier in which I hauled my field telephone equipment. We were ordered to cross the river, which could be forded at one place, take up a position in the hills and fire on a target which was too far away to reach from the battery's position. The plan was to cross the river at night, spend the day, and return the next night. We got across all right, driving in a blackout, but unfortunately that was the last thing that went as planned. It was barely an hour before daylight when we got a position set up in a little box canyon, approximately three miles from the river, and a tributary of one of the larger valleys that drained down to the river. We fired a few rounds as soon as we could. Those were the only shots we fired as long as we were there.

Before long, we heard the bugles that the Chinese always used to sound the order to attack. There was a lot of shooting over our heads, and a few mortar rounds landed in our valley, but they obviously were not shooting at us. An hour before sunrise, it sounded as though the whole Chinese army was moving past the mouth of the canyon on their way to the river. From what we could tell by listening to our radios, our tanks pulled back across the river almost immediately, and before long it was very clear to us that we were the only Americans left behind.

From time to time, we saw a few enemy soldiers on the ridges in the distance, but none of them paid any attention to us. We just dug holes and tried to stay out of sight. There was no way to conceal the guns and the trucks because they were in a cleared strip which had once been a bean field, but we piled what brush and weeds we could around them to make them a little less conspicuous. Fortunately, it was impossible to see us from the road in the main valley. We stayed in our holes for two days. Things were quiet after the second night, and amazingly, none of the enemy troops moved into our valley. On the third night, somebody decided that we would try to drive out with all our equipment. It was a good decision, for it was completely obvious that we had almost no chance of being able to walk to the river without being intercepted by the Chinese. As soon as it was completely dark, we hitched up the guns and headed out.

I was alone in my truck when we pulled out and was the last vehicle in the convoy. It was very dark, and we only used the little blackout lights on the trucks. Before long, I lost sight of the blackout lights on the ammo truck ahead of me, so I just had to trust my sense of direction and hope that I could remember all the turns in the road. I knew that there was a fork in the road, but I never spotted it, and was fortunate enough to take the correct road anyway. When I got to the river, the moon was rising, and I could see the ford quite plainly. A tractor and gun were stalled in the middle of the river. I drove out to them and stopped, and the two men in the tractor told me that everyone ahead of them had gone on, and they had not seen the ammo truck. They were quite sure they could start the tractor in a few minutes and told me to go ahead. The ford was wide enough for me to get around them, although I was worried about it. I made it across and had a relatively easy trip the last four or five miles back to our outfit. When I got there, I was met by the battery commander, who wanted to know where the hell everybody else was. I was the first one to get back!

The captain jumped in the truck with me, and we headed out to look for the others. About a mile down the road, we met the tractor that had been stalled, but did not find the rest of the convoy. About an hour after daylight, the lieutenant and his driver in the jeep accompanied by the first ammo truck showed up, followed by the other tractor and gun. They had gotten lost after crossing the river and didn't even know that the other tractor had stalled behind them. It looked as though we had lost the other ammo truck and driver, but he showed up about three days later, on foot. He had a hair-raising story to tell. He had taken a wrong turn before he got to the river and drove right into a Chinese camp. He tried to back up when they started shooting of him but of course the truck was knocked out almost immediately. He jumped out and started running, while they continued to shoot in the dark. Somehow, he made it to the brush along the riverbank and waded and swam across. He got shot at again by our guys but didn't get a scratch. He hooked up with an infantry squad, and eventually found his way back.

The ironic twist to the whole crazy episode was that while we were hiding like a bunch of scared rabbits, our outfit took a terrible pounding from artillery and had a lot of casualties. Also, when we could get up on a big hill and see the river valley in the distance, it was obvious that we had driven right by about ten thousand Chinese in the dark.

If the whole thing proves anything at all, it is that in combat, the ordinary soldier doesn't know what is happening. We knew little about the situation beyond our range of vision, but the Chinese and North Koreans probably knew even less.

Of course, I had to pull guard duty when it was my turn. Usually that was once every night for two hours, but normally we got two nights off every week. The most interesting, but also the most dangerous duty, was FO (Forward Observer). That entailed a ride up a mountain to the end of the road, then a short hike up to a specially built bunker from which there was an unobstructed view of the entire valley and the mountainside facing us. Actually, we used a BC scope to watch the landscape. It was a sort of hand-held periscope that enabled us to sit behind a parapet of sandbags under a thick roof of planks, covered with sandbags, and observe through a slit without exposing ourselves. The protection was necessary, because the observer post was exposed to small arms and machine gun fire as well as anything else the enemy could throw at us. We rotated FO duty so that no one usually had to do it more often than twice a month, for two or three days at a time. Of course, the Chinese had plenty of opportunity to zero in on the observer post, so they would drop in a mortar every now and then, and sometimes artillery. Nothing ever hit very close while I was on FO, but my good buddy Jay McClintock was hit by a white phosphorus and terribly burned while on FO. He survived but spent three years recovering in hospitals. I believe he was hit while in the trench that we used to enter the bunker, not in the bunker itself

White Phosphorus was one of the worst things you could get hit with, because even if the burns didn't kill you any phosphorus left in your body would slowly kill you anyway. I have always felt guilty about Jay being hit, because I was scheduled for the FO when he was wounded, but he volunteered to take my place. I vividly remember the morning he left to go up to the FO post. I was up and ready to go to the post at 3:00 A.M. Unexpectedly, Jay was also up and by the dim light of a flashlight in the bunker he told me he would take my place. I told him, no, I would go, and asked him why he wanted to trade. He said it was because I was scheduled to leave the outfit in a few more weeks, and since I was married and had a kid, he thought I didn't need to take any more chances. I said OK, and he left. Maybe we both had a premonition that my luck was running out.

Back of the picture reads: "Left to right, Yours truly, Don Stevens. Berthoud, Colo. Charlie ("Lew") Herchanhon Baltimore, Md. Jay McClintock, Paramus, N.J., Dick Carey, Eugene, Ore.

Left to right,
Yours truly,
Don Stevens, Berthoud, Colo.
Charlie ("Lew") Herchanhan
Baltimore, Md.
Jay McClintock, Paramus, N.J.
Dick Carey. Eugene, Ore.

The weather soon turned cold. Fog covered the landscape almost every morning. In fact, most mornings were foggy even in the summer and it hung on longer in the winter. We got some snow too. It snowed frequently, but not very much at a time. I thought I was used to cold weather from growing up in northern Iowa, but the dampness made the cold more penetrating, and working outside became increasingly more uncomfortable. We didn't have enough winter clothing. Many of us had none. None of us came into Korea with anything but summer clothing, and very few warm garments made it as far as North Korea while we were there. Whenever anyone left the outfit, he left any cold weather gear that he might have acquired to those who stayed behind. That was the way I got what little warm clothing I had. There was a serious shortage of socks. In one of my letters to Arlene I mentioned that I needed socks very badly, and she sent me several pairs in the mail. Believe me, they were a lifesaver. Keeping a pair of socks pinned under my shirt was the only way to ensure that I had a reasonably dry pair to change into. Everybody did that. It was the only way to avoid frostbitten feet because our boots were seldom dry.

We bought winter caps from the English and Canadians and boots from the Australians when we got a chance. Shortly before I left Charlie Battery, I acquired a fur-trimmed cap from somewhere. I don't remember how I got it, but I remember what a luxury it was to have a warm cap. Before that, I also had a wool beret that I got from a Canadian that was a lot warmer that the GI fatigue cap I was issued. Nobody cared if we wore those odds and ends of non-regulation gear if we were careful not to wear them outside our battery area. I always wanted a pair of Australian boots, but never got any. They were not really cold weather gear but were much better than our GI boots. The Canadians had waterproof insulated boots, real Arctic footwear, but would not part with them. In short, while North Korea is certainly a chilly place in the winter, the lack of winter clothing made it much worse. I was quite sick for a few days about that time, with a recurrence of the same illness I had earlier. Our medic in the battalion thought I might have malaria, which was unusual in Korea. Whenever I had an attack, it would come on very suddenly. I lost a lot of weight from those episodes.

Shortly after that, our battery was pulled back into reserve. By that time, we were seriously shorthanded, having lost quite a few men through casualties, and more because their term of service was ending. The reserve time was incredibly boring. More booze was available than we ever saw up north and drinking was the only recreation. There was a lot of drinking going on. We lived in tents that were all set up for us. They even had wooden floors and wooden frames that kept them neatly squared up. There was even a shower-- the first I had seen since I arrived in Korea! We were issued new winter coats too. I remember feeling a little bitter about that, because I didn't need it nearly as much as I had needed it when I was in the combat zone and couldn't get one. We were supposed to be undergoing training, but no one took it very seriously. We did have a competitive shooting match. For once in my army days, I drew a good rifle, and I won first place with the highest score in the battalion. Maybe that was because of my plinking days back on the farm, or perhaps as my buddies suggested someone else was so bad, they were shooting at my target! I even got a chance to take a day off and visit Seoul, which turned out to be a very drab, dirty, bombed-out, but still heavily populated city, hardly what could be called a tourist attraction.

The return to polished boots and pointless details was irritating too. I soon realized that I was a lot more at home with the combat environment where nobody gave a damn what you looked like, just that you could be trusted to do your job. I very soon settled down to counting the days until I could go home.

I left Charlie Battery in December 1952. After a cold ride in the back of a truck to Inchon, on the shore of the Yellow Sea, we spent a night in a little camp that was right in a town. It gave me a glimpse of how the

Korean civilians lived. That was really a novelty because we never saw civilians most of the time I was in Korea. It was a lot warmer in Inchon than it had been where we had been before. The thing I remember most about Inchon is the stinking mile-wide mudflat that is exposed at low tide. We boarded a landing craft (LST) for the trip out to the ship about five miles offshore. From the LST we had to climb a rope ladder to board the ship. The ship was rolling enough so that the ladder would alternately drop about six feet and swing away from the ship, then pull up a corresponding distance and swing toward the ship. The trick was to grab the ladder on the lowest part of the swing, and then hang on as you were jerked over the side of the landing craft and banged against the side of the ship. We were carrying full field packs, so it was not an easy climb, but everybody made it. The ship was the General Howze, the same ship on which I crossed the Pacific the first time. There were not a lot of us getting on at Inchon so we had lots of room on the three-day voyage to Sasebo, on the southern tip of Japan.

I got sick again at Sasebo, but I refused to go on sick call because I was afraid that if I did, I would be put in a hospital and be stuck there for a while. I was determined to get home as fast as I could. We had to turn in every scrap of clothing, and any odds and ends we brought from Korea. The initial uniform I was issued was too small for me. I stepped on a scale for the first time since I left the U.S. and got a big surprise. I had weighed 170 when I left Ft. Riley but was now down to only 135 pounds. I was feeling a little better by the time we got back on the ship but was still a little weak. In fact, while I would never admit it, I had lost a lot of strength from the time I first got sick and couldn't seem to get it back.

The trip home was a lot rougher than the trip going across. We hit a lot of bad weather and got food poisoning from a bad batch of turkey that we had for Christmas dinner. Believe me, an outbreak of food poisoning on a crowded troopship is a very bad situation. I got sick but not as bad as many did. One soldier died, and I heard that the sick bay was full for over a week.

Finally, after three weeks crossing the Pacific, we pulled into Seattle. The harbor was shrouded in a dense fog, so it was impossible to see the city. When we finally pulled into the pier, many of us were out on deck, packed like sardines, of course, but every one of us willing to put up with some discomfort just to get the first glimpse of the U. S. again. There was a long caravan of GI buses waiting to take us to Ft. Lewis, and a couple of ladies at the bottom of the gangplank wishing each of us welcome home. Aside from that, nobody in Seattle seemed to notice us at all. After a short bus ride to Ft. Lewis, we were processed through with astonishing speed. It was the most efficient job of handling a large number of troops I ever experienced while I was in the army. We had tied up at the pier just a little while after dawn, and before dark I had finished processing and was on a train headed for Camp Carson, near Colorado Springs. The Pullman car on the train seemed like unbelievable luxury to me after what I had just experienced. It was an enjoyable trip.

Processing for discharge was the usual hurry-up and wait routine. Before I was separated from active service, I got a weekend pass. Obsessed by the desire to get home, I hopped on a bus to Denver, and took a train to Boone, Iowa, where Arlene met me. After a short visit, I took my car and drove back to Colorado, which was a mistake. I got caught in a blizzard in western Nebraska, and barely made it back to camp before I would have been AWOL. On January 16, 1953 I was formally transferred from active duty to the enlisted reserve and left my Army days behind.

25

Half A Century

Fifty years sounds like an awfully long time. Now that the 50th anniversary of our marriage has come and gone, it seems appropriate to take a look at that half-century. The dates are July 28,1951-July 28,2001, but those dates don't tell the story at all. All the important things are represented by the dash between them. Every year seems to go faster than the last, so fifty years have slipped away more quickly than I ever could have imagined. Of course, it is impossible to remember everything that happened during that time, but every major event is burned into our memories as well as a great many things that were relatively trivial. This is a personal history. I am not attempting to confine it to memories that include both of us, but almost everything has been influenced by the fact that Arlene and I were married.

Married July 28, 1951

26

Fort Riley, Kansas

The circumstances at the time of our marriage were unusual. I was in the Army stationed at Fort Riley, Kansas. I was an instructor in the field wireman school there. In my case, that meant I was teaching basic electrical theory. This was during the Korean War and there was heavy fighting going on there. Now for the unusual part--that year in northeastern Kansas and southeastern Nebraska the rains came, and they wouldn't stop. All through June the ground was saturated, and the rivers were running high, then in July it rained a whole lot more. Camp Funston, the part of Ft. Riley where I was stationed, was in a flood plain. The river crested about 13 feet higher than the levee, which was supposed to protect the camp. Thousands of soldiers had to move out into the hills on very short notice.

Suddenly, the dozen or so of us guys who had been teaching how to set up and operate a field telephone system had to really do it. We started working a couple of hours before the troops were evacuated but had no chance to pack any clothes or gear (such as pup tents) that we would normally take. We had lots of telephone equipment, but otherwise all we had were the clothes we put on that day. For the next five days, we worked day and night. Finally, the water went down enough that two of us, Bill O'Quinn and I, were able to wade along highway 40 and hook up with working telephone lines out of Junction City. By doing so we activated the first outside line available since the camp was flooded. What did all of this have to do with getting married? All of this happened the week before the wedding was scheduled, so about the time I should have been marching down the aisle, I was still isolated with no hope of going anywhere and no way to call home.

We did get married, only a week late, and went to live in Kansas. It was nearly impossible to find a decent place to live in Manhattan, Iowa so we went through a period of living in crummy furnished rooms, but then finally got a nice little apartment. When Arlene got pregnant and was sick, she went back home for a while. I mistakenly thought she probably would be gone for a long time, let the apartment go and moved back to the base. I was wrong. Before long she was ready to come back, and I had to find another place. That was hard to do because of the flood damage, but I did find a small apartment in an old house. It wasn't great, but we managed. Arlene even did a good job of baking with an antiquated gas range. The oven on that beast was either on the highest heat or off, with no control of the temperature in between!

About that time, Pearl Pedersen, Arlene's cousin, moved in with us while her husband, Cecil, was in basic training. We didn't have much money, but we had a lot of fun. The girls were expert at stretching our grocery money to the limit. What was not fun was the fact that Arlene was pregnant, and often very sick. Pearl was pregnant too!

On the very day our son David was born in the Army hospital, I got my orders to ship out to Korea. When he was only a week old, we packed him and everything we owned into our little Plymouth and drove back home. After a few days there, I was off to California on a train, and before long I was in the middle of a war in North Korea.

In the fall, Arlene took a job teaching in a country school not far from her parent's farm. It was not difficult for her to get a job because she already had five years of teaching experience. During the time we were dating she taught 3rd grade at West Bend, Iowa, and before that she taught all eight grades in a country school near Joice, Iowa, and West Maple Grove School near Bode, Iowa. She was a wonderful teacher and loved working with kids. She used this talent for most of her adult life and always loved the profession. While I was overseas, she and David alternated between living with her parents and my parents.

When I returned to Iowa after the end of my active military service, we had to face some urgent questions. I knew I wanted to farm, but I had no land.

27

Bode, Iowa

We had no place of our own to live, and naturally assumed that we would have to find a farm where we could live as well as plant crops. We started looking immediately, and within a month we discovered an opportunity to rent a small farm with an old house in Arlene's home community.

We started farming on that 80-acre farm near Bode, Iowa. It was too small to support a family, although we tried to make it more profitable by raising cattle and hogs and milking cows. The buildings on the farm were old, and the house was not very good. The well was not good, so our water supply was questionable at best. That farm provided a place to get established and give us time to look for something better, but it wasn't big enough to provide sufficient income for a family. I used the tractor I had stored while I was in the service. I bought most of the rest of my machinery at farm sales. I didn't have enough money to buy new or good used machinery, so I tried to get along with old worn-out junk. Most of the time this old stuff worked, but often it did a poor job. Even though I was a pretty good mechanic, I wasted a lot of time and effort fixing things and still got unsatisfactory results. This was a problem that eventually cost me money and got me in trouble with my landlords. In fact, that first year my old corn picker left so much corn in the field that my landlord was unhappy because he didn't get as much corn as he thought he should have. Worse yet, I tried to salvage what I could by pasturing the stalks. One cow died, and others got sick from eating too much corn. It was an expensive lesson, one that I have never forgotten. I never used that old picker again.

We looked for another place, and succeeded in renting 160 acres northwest of Algona, Iowa near the little town of Lone Rock. We moved from the Bode area to the Lone Rock farm in March 1954. We usually referred to the community as Lone Rock, even though our mail address was Algona.

28

Lone Rock, Iowa

Arlene was pregnant again before we moved. She was even sicker throughout the pregnancy than she had been with David and was hospitalized several times. Paul was born in the Algona hospital when David was two years old. Their birthdays were only three days apart.

Farming was a little better on that place, but we were still scratching out a rather meager living at best. Once again, the machinery problem came up. My planter was worn out, and my farm manager decreed that unless I bought a new planter, I would lose the lease on the farm. Of course, I bought a new planter whether I could afford it or not. I bought a better corn picker, and a good combine too. All the time we were there I was building up my dairy herd until it became my main livestock enterprise.

At the time we moved to that farm the house was so old and run-down that it was hardly fit to live in. The ceilings were falling, the plaster was falling off the walls, and the roof leaked all over. It was almost impossible to heat in the winter. In cold weather, Paul slept in our bed. When Arlene put a bottle on the floor by the bed after feeding him during the night, the remaining milk would be frozen solid by morning. When we moved in there was a two-by-four propping up the ceiling in the living room to keep it from falling. We had to put Paul's crib in the kitchen because we were afraid the ceiling in the other part of the house would fall on him. We patched the walls with cardboard. I can remember sitting at the table eating and looking at the Carnation Milk boxes nailed up on the wall.

Sometime in the fall I bought a roll of the red rosin Kraft paper used in building, intending to cover the foundation and lower outside walls so I could pile straw bales against the house to stop some of the winter winds. The next day I was busy at the neighbors filling their silo, and when I got home, I found that Arlene had redecorated! She tore off the Carnation boxes and covered the walls with the paper and nailed up wood laths to hold it in place. It really looked quite nice. In fact, the landlord remarked the next time he visited that it looked so good that perhaps he wouldn't have to build a new house!

Arlene was an active partner in farming in those days. She could drive a tractor if necessary and give me a hand when I was doing anything that I couldn't possibly do by myself. In the spring when we sowed oats, she drove the tractor while I was in the wagon with our two little kids and shoveled the seed into the seeder. In the summer, she hauled grain in from the combine, and in the fall, she hauled corn and unloaded it as I ran the picker. She could milk the cows and feed the livestock if she had to, although I usually did not need to call on her to help with the chores.

Of course, the housework was not easy. The water from the well was not fit to drink, so we had to haul all the water for drinking and cooking from a neighboring farm. In fact, the water was loaded with sulfur and stunk so bad when it first was pumped out of the well that the cattle would not drink it until it had aired out for several hours. We did have a bathroom, though, supplied from a cistern that was replenished with the water from the well. Eventually, our landlord, Mr. Haden, drilled a new well so we had a good water supply the last few months we lived there.

Mr. Haden decided that he would build a new house, and then tried to change his mind. I say he tried, because Arlene and I tore the old house down as soon as he said he would build a new one, so that when he arrived with the intention of patching up the old house, he found it was almost gone. We lived in the one remaining room while he built the new house around it.

When the job was finally finished, Mr. Haden acknowledged that we had done the right thing by tearing the old house down, and that he would have been better off if he had not attempted to save any of it. The room he saved was the original cabin, which apparently was built in the 1860's. The lumber in it was rough sawed yellow pine. I found the material in the old cabin interesting, because it was of such a high quality. In the process of razing the various additions that had been built later than the original cabin, we found old newspapers, some originals as old as 1878 and reprints--including one from the time of Lincoln's assassination in 1865. Judging from the newspapers we found inside the wall, which were apparently pasted there to make the wall more airtight, we guessed that the last addition was built in 1878.

Arlene and I did some of the drywall finishing and all the interior painting. We enjoyed the new house. It was a tremendous improvement. We lived on that farm three years.

In 1956 Cheryl was born. The pregnancy was not as bad as when Arlene was carrying Paul, but the delivery was very difficult. Arlene was in labor for a week and when Cheryl was finally born, she came breech, and Arlene hemorrhaged severely, so badly that we almost lost her.

David loved the farm when he was a little boy. He was with me every time he had a chance, particularly when I was milking or working with the cattle. Paul liked it too but didn't have as much of a chance to enjoy it before we left the farm. David knew every cow by name, watched every detail of calving and veterinary work, and tried to help any way he could. I particularly remember one New Year's Eve when one of my heifers was calving. David was with me each time I checked her. After a while, I realized that the calf was not in the normal position and decided that I had better call the vet. Even though it was getting late, David wanted to watch while we worked and finally succeeded in delivering the calf. Finally, after the vet had left and we were sure that the calf was going to be all right, I carried David into the house and put him to bed. He was a very tired little boy, but he was happy.

Me, Paul, the toy tractor, David, Arlene and our farm

29

Lu Verne, Iowa

Our next move was to a farm owned by my father, near LuVerne, Iowa. We moved there during the winter of 1956-57. By that time, I had dropped all the livestock activities except milking and raising Holstein cattle. We had to build a new building for a milking parlor before we could move, because the barn was never set up for milking and was in poor condition.

The first year there went well. While the house was small, it was in good condition, and we lived comfortably even though we didn't have much room. The kids were very happy there. Arlene helped a lot with the chores of keeping the milk room and the milking machines clean, and even helped with the milking and feeding when she could. She did our laundry in the milk room too, because there was no place to do it in the house. David and Paul were outside every chance they had and spent a lot of time with me. Cheryl was still quite small, but she was good natured and easy to take care of and enjoyed being with the boys. Arlene occasionally did some substitute teaching in LuVerne. David started school in LuVerne, walking more than a quarter mile to and from the bus every day. I had my share of problems with the cows but managed to keep my head above water most of the time.

The spring of 1958 was a very bad time for us. Even now I do not like to write about it. I ran out of hay and had to start buying it in the early spring. Of course, that was an expense, but worse, it was very difficult to load and unload it because of muddy yards, and of course feeding was a tough job because of the mud. The cows suffered because of the mud, too. Before long I had an epidemic of mastitis (udder infection) on my hands.

This was the situation that faced me on the morning of Good Friday, 1958. A cold rain was falling. I was getting sick. We were almost out of hay again and several cows had mastitis. Before long, I realized I had the mumps. By midmorning, I was so sick I had to go in the house and go to bed. That was the last time I was able to work for three months or more. The next three weeks were a continuing nightmare. Paul also had the mumps. Both of us were very sick. I suffered for a while at home, and then had to go to the hospital. Not only did I have the mumps; I apparently also had viral meningitis. I felt like I was near death, and I was almost completely blind. My eyesight started to come back after about eight days of almost total blindness, but the recovery was slow, and I never again was able to see as well as I could before.

Meanwhile, Arlene was having a terrible time. Paul was very sick while I was in the hospital. She had to buy hay and arrange to get it delivered. One of our best cows died the day I went to the hospital. She had to do lot of the chores herself because it was hard to get help, and of course she had to take care of Paul and the other kids. Both my family and hers helped, but she still had a very heavy burden.

After I got out of the hospital, I still had a long slow recovery ahead. Even though I was working again in mid-summer, I still wasn't able to do a good day's work for a long time. By that time our milk production was way down and never did come back to what it was before.

Relatively speaking, the crops did better that year than the livestock since our two families helped to take care of the fieldwork until I could do it myself, but undoubtedly things may have turned out better if I hadn't been sick. I was so discouraged that nothing looked good to me anymore.

The rest of the year was better, but the damage was done. After we got the crops harvested, I was faced with the toughest decision of my life. I could keep on farming or find some other way to make a living.

30

Farmington, New Mexico

The Point, David, Cheryl, Paul and Arlene

Arlene and I decided we should take a trip and get away for a few days. We had a good car, so we didn't consider any way to go other than driving. We made the necessary arrangements and hit the road, not at all sure where or how far we would go. Looking back now, for me it was an act of desperation. Regardless of what our banker, our families, and our friends had to say, I could not see any reason for us to go on with what we had been doing. I am sure that Arlene was more optimistic than I was, but she could be persuaded to go along with whatever I chose to do-- but only if she thought it was a good idea. In fact, she has always had an adventurous streak as well, and enjoyed the challenge of going somewhere she had never been and making a fresh new start.

It was winter in Iowa and the weather was cold and dreary, so it was only natural for us to go toward the southwest to look for sunshine and warmer temperatures. Our journey took us to Nebraska then Kansas, then southern Colorado. We wanted to see some mountains, so we went over Wolf Creek Pass to Durango. Then looking of the map we decided we were so close to New Mexico we should see a little of that, so we went to Aztec. I vividly remember stopping in Aztec to eat. It was the middle of December, the sky was crystal clear, the sun was warm, and it just felt wonderful! There was a four-lane highway leading to Farmington, so we decided to go there. One of the things that we both felt at that time was that we did not want to go to a big city. Contrary to any logical reason, I was fascinated by being in a community that compared to the Midwest was in many ways an outpost on the frontier. The Four Corners country was, and still is, a remarkable region of vast and sparsely inhabited high desert, beautiful in its own way. Farmington was a boom town, still going through the growing pains of being transformed in a few short years from being a little farming and trading town on the edge of the Navajo reservation to an exploding city, the center of the vast San Juan Basin oil and gas field. It was civilized enough to be comfortable and still close enough to its pioneer past to be an exciting and fun place to live. We liked what we saw, and from that moment on we were hooked.

Before we left Farmington, I interviewed for a job at Mountain Bell Telephone Company and was assured that I would have a good chance of getting a job when I came back. We signed a contract to buy a house in Farmington, and then went home to wind up our farming career. It was hard to break the news to our parents that we were quitting. It was a terrible disappointment to them, but we had made our decision and stuck to it. I know that some of our friends and neighbors predicted we would be back in a year or two, but I never felt that we would do that.

We had an auction on January 6, 1959, and sold everything except our car, household necessities, our clothing, and some furniture. It was a painful experience to see the machinery and tools we had worked so hard to buy and the cattle that I had tended for countless hours all sold and scattered in just a few hours. Naturally, we had to pay off the bank, but got enough from the sale to get out of debt and have a few dollars left over.

When it was over, we all cried when the last truckload of cattle went down the lane. We all loved living on the farm despite the hardships and it was hard to let it go.

Moving Day, Paul, Arlene, Cheryl, David and Me

The big move would have been stressful enough without illness, but we weren't so lucky. David came down with a bad case of measles while we were on the road and was terribly sick when we went through Kansas. Finally, we arrived in Farmington and moved into our new house, a week before our furniture arrived. Within an hour or two, we discovered what wonderful new neighbors we had. They started to come over to meet us, and when they found we had no furniture, they brought over a card table and chairs and a few other things so we could eat and sleep until our furniture arrived. All of them were newcomers as well, mostly from Texas, and they were eager to make new friends. Within an incredibly short time, we were accepted into this brand-new community, and many of those great people became lifelong friends.

I started work for Mountain Bell within a couple of weeks as a temporary employee. On March 1, 1959, I was hired as a regular employee and I remained an employee of Ma Bell for the next 27 years.

Very soon after that I was on my way to work one morning when the driver of the car behind me honked his horn and motioned me to pull over. Of course, I had no idea what was going on, but there was no other traffic and he looked friendly, so I pulled over and stopped. He got out of his car, came over and introduced himself. He was Charlie Anderson. Of course, that meant nothing to me, but he explained that he saw the Iowa license on my car, and since he had moved from Iowa himself a short time before, he wanted to meet me. His wife Gladys was a teacher. While we have lived hundreds of miles apart for most of the last 40 years, we have always kept in touch and counted them as friends. They had two boys, the younger of whom, Dean, was about the same age as our Paul. When they were old enough to start kindergarten, there was a question--where would those boys go to kindergarten? There was no kindergarten in the public school then.

The answer came almost as soon as the question was asked. Arlene and Gladys would start their own. At first, they intended to use the Anderson's house but that did not work out well, so Arlene volunteered the use of our house, set about getting the license and all the necessary permits, and Cinderella Kindergarten was born. Gladys took a job teaching in a nearby high school in the fall and dropped out of the kindergarten venture soon afterwards. For the rest of the time we lived in Farmington, our house did double duty. It was a both a home and a schoolhouse. That meant that we had a very strict routine. Everybody had to get up early, pick things up, make the beds, clean the bathrooms as well as get ready for school and work. Everybody had a job; the kids did their part, so the system worked very smoothly. The house was ready for inspection every day, and when the state inspector did drop in, there was never a problem.

The kids in kindergarten did well too, and the parents were always pleased. There was never any problem with collecting the monthly fee. In short, even though it was a small operation at first, it was always successful. Arlene never needed to advertise after the kindergarten got going. As time went on, she got all the kids she could handle. She always included lots of music, as well as teaching the basic skills. She put on an operetta each year, which was a truly polished performance. Those kids learned every word and note and sang very well considering their age. The parents got into the act by making costumes, some of which were truly works of art. I built stage sets and props. One of those I remember best was a grandfather clock built to fit the little boy who had the part of the "Obliging Clock." Those operettas were great fun for everybody, and I can honestly say I have never seen children's performance that was any better.

Arlene's Cinderella Kindergarten operetta, featuring the "Obliging Clock"

Of course, not everything went as well as the kindergarten. Arlene came down with rheumatic fever the first year we were in Farmington, and never had the privilege of being hospitalized when she should have been or being able to rest at home as much as she should have, because the kids were still small and demanded her attention. Quite probably the inadequate rest while she had the acute stage of rheumatic fever contributed to the heart problems, she has had most of her life. She recovered slowly. As a matter of fact, she was not completely recovered when I came down with the same disease a year later. My case was handled better. I was in the hospital for a little while, and then had bed rest at home for weeks.

When I was back on my feet, the doctor said I had no permanent damage, but I know better. For a while afterwards I had pains, moderately severe at times, which were the same as the angina I had about 38 years later before my bypass surgery. I thought I was too young to have heart trouble and blamed the pain on other things. I know Arlene had pain too.

The other major event of our first year in Farmington was when our first house went to pieces. Of course, we should not have bought before we knew the soil conditions and the builder's reputation, but we bought anyway, and suffered the consequences. San Medina was a street that traversed the face of a rather steep hill. Our house was on the downhill side of the street. What we did not know was that while the lot had been terraced so that it was level, the underlying rock was a steeply tilted sheet of sandstone. In fact, after the lot was graded, there were only eighteen inches of soil over the bedrock at the curb, but fourteen feet of fill dirt at the rear of the house. When we started to water the lawn the settling and sliding began and it went fast. We moved in February. By September the house was pulling apart. We had complained to the builder almost continually since we first saw cracks, but he ignored it.

When things got to the point where the interior partition between the kitchen and living room was four inches off the floor, and the water heater had to be shut off because the vent had pulled apart making a four-inch gap in the pipe, I called the city building inspector. I was at work when he came, but I heard later that he walked in, looked at the house very briefly, went back to his truck, picked up a "condemned" sign and nailed it to the front door. Finally, that got the builder's attention.

He was still building houses in the neighborhood, and he had one that was completed but not sold. He offered to trade even up, and we accepted. It was a larger house and better floor plan than the other was. Of course, it was on the same hillside, just one street farther up, but we had to move out immediately and had to make a quick decision. The builder pulled a framing crew off the job, sent them over with a flatbed truck, and moved us in to the other house. We had no time to pack, so we simply carried a lot of the little stuff, but despite everything we came through with very little damage or loss. All things considered; it was not a bad deal at all. We lived in that house on San Paula all the rest of our stay in Farmington.

The kids adapted to our new style of living quite quickly, although David was very homesick for the farm at first. There were other kids in the neighborhood about the same age, and before long they had lots of friends to play with. We always remember little Diana Warren who lived down the hill from us. She was the same age as Paul, and when she first met him, she rushed home to tell her mother excitedly: "There's this new boy and he has the prettiest whitest hair!" The funny part was that she was a little cutie too and had the same shade of platinum blonde hair as Paul.

David started at Ladera Del Norte School as soon as we arrived in town. Paul and Cheryl went through kindergarten and started at the same school when they were old enough. They were all very good students from the very beginning. Arlene was elected president of the PTA and was always in close touch with happenings at school. We adopted a Cocker Spaniel dog too. Perhaps it would be just as accurate to say he adopted us. In any case, as soon as he showed up in the neighborhood, Boots was Paul's buddy, and he was our family companion for the rest of his life. He was an exceptionally smart dog, and the kids had a lot of fun with him. He traveled with us on our long trips, and long distance moves as well.

Paul and Boots

David started delivering papers and was very successful with his paper route. When he was old enough to enter science fairs, he always did an ambitious project, and usually won a high award. Paul and Cheryl did some neat projects at their own grade level, too. Often those projects, such as the model of a Navajo hogan, involved Arlene and me before they were finished. Paul and David both played Little League baseball and Cheryl took dance lessons. She showed a lot of talent in gymnastics and starred in dance recitals by performing some highly athletic routines with a boy.

As the kids grew, they loved going out in the hills near our house and exploring. Once, David and one of his friends met me as I got home from work, and excitedly informed me that they had found the neatest piece of petrified wood, and they wanted me to haul it home and put it in the yard. I went with them to look at it, and indeed it was a neat piece. It was a petrified stump and must have weighed at least half a ton. Naturally, it stayed right where they uncovered it.

One of our favorite Sunday afternoon activities in those days was exploring. We didn't have to go far. We could start within a block or two from our house, but our best excursions were when we took the car and drove north towards Mesa Verde. We found sites where the ground was littered with shards of broken Anasazi pottery, probably 1000 years old. One of those sites was a fire pit that was probably used for centuries where the ashes were mixed with small animal and bird bones and potshards to a depth of several feet. There were pit houses too, long since filled with sand, but they were typically at lower elevations out on the desert south of the San Juan River. I often encountered them when I was patrolling the toll line.

A day in the desert

A couple of our friends who we met in church operated a trading post in Arizona on the Navajo reservation. We soon discovered that they had hand-woven Navajo rugs for sale, and for a few years we bought some and gave them away as Christmas presents because they were so cheap, not keeping any for ourselves. Since then, they have become very scarce and valuable. We still have one in the family that my parents left to us. Another artifact that Cheryl still has is a cradleboard made by a Navajo woman that our friends gave to Cheryl. These things are a cherished reminder of the time when our family was growing up near the reservation.

Arlene first joined a sorority when we were in Farmington. The women seemed to have a lot of fun, and occasionally they would throw a party and invite the husbands too. I remember a particularly good Halloween costume party. The Flintstones were very popular on TV then, so our neighbor and friend Pigeon Stevens convinced us to go as Fred and Wilma Flintstone. Arlene made the costumes and Pigeon did our makeup. We won first prize!

During the first couple of years in Farmington, before Arlene started to make money on her kindergarten and I got a pay raise or two, money was a little scarce in our house. For a while I moonlighted at another job to make ends meet, working in a liquor store and the bar attached to it, but it was a tough way to live. I hated it and quit as soon as we could make it without the extra few dollars.

Unfortunately, the oil-drilling boom ended in the first half of the 1960's so the economy and the real estate values went into a downward spiral.

Farmington was a fun place to live at that time, despite all the difficulties. Many of the people who lived there would have had a hard time living in a suburban community where everything is covenant controlled and everybody is expected to conform to the community rules.

On our street, our next-door neighbor, Royce (Mac) McKissick bought an old Link Trainer (an early flight simulator used to train pilots for flying with instruments). It was a basket case when he hauled it home from Georgia. He reassembled it in his garage, and when the time came to work on the electrical circuits, he enlisted my help. It was a challenge. The circuit diagrams covered about a half dozen large sheets of paper. The wires were jammed into a cardboard box, all tangled up with no attempt to preserve any identification. Of course, they were all color coded and cut to the proper length, but even then, identifying the individual circuits and making at least a hundred or more connections correctly was a big job. Finally, it was done, and it worked. The big electric fan, which furnished the air pressure and simulated the noise of a real airplane, went outside--right under our bedroom window. Mac was the tower chief at the airport, so he had a captive clientele of pilots who were willing to buy a few hours under the hood, to get, or retain their instrument ratings. Often those hours were racked up at night, so we had to get used to sleeping with that roaring monster just a few feet away. For my reward, I was allowed to spend a few hours under the hood myself, which was enough to convince me I was not ever going to be a pilot.

Meanwhile, I was building a tractor in my garage. I had to do a good deal of welding, which probably could have disturbed the neighbors, but no one ever complained. I also did some welding for my friends who were building projects of their own. One of those was our neighbor Bill Floyd, living a couple of doors down the street, who was building an airplane in his garage. He had very few tools with which to work. He bought the plans for a proven experimental design and modified them by building a slightly longer wing and installing a bigger engine to adapt the plane for takeoffs and landings at high altitude airports. The airframe was all wood covered with fabric, typical for light aircraft then. My involvement was confined to making some parts for the landing gear, which he found in a salvage yard, and drilling a few holes in other metal parts. He kept the plane out of sight for the most part during the year it took to build, but when he finally installed the motor and propeller, he could not resist the temptation to start it. The wings were completed but he could not install them until he moved the plane to the airport. He moved the airplane minus wings out on his front lawn, tied the tail wheel to his little tree, chocked the wheels and started the engine. All went well until he revved the engine just a little too much. It was too much for the tree. The plane nosed over and dug the prop into the grass. Nobody was hurt, but the prop and the tree too were beyond saving.

That might have discouraged a lesser man, but my neighbor did not let that bother him. Soon afterward, he moved the plane to the airport, where with a new prop he began testing the plane. The first taxiing test revealed that the craft was nose heavy, requiring that the landing gear be moved forward. The mechanic who was inspecting the plane didn't like the gear anyway, so Bill found a different landing gear, and I helped a little in installing it. Finally, the plane passed all the inspections and was ready for flight-testing. It took a little fine tuning, requiring the addition of a little weight in the tail to compensate for being nose heavy in flight, but with that correction, it flew very well. The Floyds moved to Oklahoma soon afterward. After a little while we lost touch with them, but I have often wondered about the history of that airplane.

Meanwhile, I finished my little tractor. It was a success, but the only use we had for it was for the kids to play with. They had a great time with it and spent many hours driving it.

Duane Becker and his wife Eleanor lived a few blocks from us, and we became good friends. Eleanor, whom we knew by her nickname of Sis, is a very talented artist. Duane and I spent a lot of time working on his various projects, as well as going on hunting trips every year. Duane was a good shadetree mechanic, however, it seemed as though every year when we ventured out into the middle of nowhere on a hunting trip, we always had trouble with his vehicle. Of course, we always took both his jeep and my pickup whenever we went out, so we were never stranded, but twice I had to tow his jeep home, well over a hundred miles each time. Our favorite hunting ground was the Jicarilla Apache Indian reservation. It is rugged and remote, mostly unpopulated, a great place to hunt but a terrible place to have a vehicle break down, forty miles of rough trail from the nearest paved road, and even farther from any settlement. Hunting there was severely limited, but we applied for permits every year and usually got them. I was more interested in exploring the wild land of pinon and sage, mesas, and deep canyons than in hunting. Once out there, we hardly ever saw another human being.

We never tired of exploring the diverse backgrounds and varied interests of the people in our part of Farmington as well as the stark beauty of the land. Arlene had many delightful friends and we enjoyed good times with them. There were a lot of kids about the same age as ours, so we got acquainted with them and their parents as well. Harold and Gertie Greiner moved from Iowa shortly after we did, and we became friends almost immediately. Rather than hiring a moving company, they moved all their stuff in the truck Harold and his partner owned in Iowa, so they had no help to move into the house. Remembering how good our neighbors were to us when we first arrived, I helped carry in their furniture.

All through this period we were quite active in church. When we first started attending the Lutheran church, it was a tiny congregation meeting in an old building almost exactly like the one-room country schools we attended when we were kids. I was the Sunday school superintendent and Arlene taught classes. It was tough finding a place to hold our Sunday school classes. First, we tried to manage by meeting in homes. Later we had the opportunity to use a medical clinic building. That was not an ideal arrangement, but it worked for a while. Still later, in 1963, we built a new church. It was small, but a pretty little church, nevertheless. I was on the church council at the time and remember a few battles we went through while planning and building. Even though our congregation was a mission church, we didn't have a whole lot of money to work with. It was a constant struggle to keep the building cost within the budget. I have always felt we got good value for our money, thanks in part to the volunteers who helped whenever they could.

About this time, I started singing again. Despite my singing experience when I was younger, I had dropped it altogether for quite a few years. Largely because there were so few who volunteered to sing, I started again in the church choir in Farmington, and before long was singing in a mixed quartet as well. I also was involved in an attempt to start a barbershop quartet with three guys who were fathers of David's friends. That quartet had possibilities, but soon one or two of them moved away, and left soon afterward. My very last social activity in Farmington was singing with our mixed quartet for a Rainbow Girls installation on January 1, 1965. I left the next day for Socorro, and never worked in Farmington again.

During the years we were in Farmington, I had many different job assignments within the telephone company. All of them were in the Plant department. Most of the time when I changed job titles, I moved to a higher rated job, but not always. I worked in the warehouse for a very short time, and then moved up to installer-repairman for a while. When I got rheumatic fever and had to take sick leave, it was a temporary setback. When I reported for work again, I was assigned as a frameman, a less strenuous job, working in the switchroom. That was a lower rated job, but it was a good learning experience. From there I moved to plant line assignor. That was strictly an office job, but once again it was a good learning step. In the Farmington office we overlapped tasks quite a lot, so on a given day I would probably assign some orders, go out and help the frameman make the connections, and quite possibly man the testboard while the testboardman was at lunch. Before long, I was ready to work outside again and went back to the installer repairman job. I enjoyed all of it.

Me and David, at work

During my second stint as an installer-repairman, I started working toll patrol part of the time. That wasn't just a job; it could be an adventure. The job was to maintain several hundred miles of telephone wire, which was strung on poles across the desert. For me, it meant that sometimes I was working a portion of the Durango-Gallup line. Our section extended from the state line between Durango and Aztec, to a trading post at Newcomb, New Mexico, which is about halfway between Shiprock and Gallup. Other times, I might be working the Angel's Peak repeater line, which extended from Farmington to a tower on a mountain southeast of Bloomfield.

The one that I remember best, though, was the Aneth line. It was a decrepit old line that was originally built for the Bureau of Indian affairs to serve trading posts on the reservation. At the time I patrolled it, the BIA leased it to El Paso Natural Gas Co., in turn Mountain Bell was contracted to maintain it for EPNG. Normally, Mountain Bell people did not cross state lines, but since this was a contract job, it was an exception. The route started at Shiprock, about thirty miles from Farmington. From there it extended to Tees Nos Pas, AZ. The Aneth line continued north and east from there to the crossing of the San Juan River, near the Four Corners. From there, it was in Colorado for a few miles, then westward into Utah. From there, it meandered through some very rugged country to Aneth, Utah, 205 miles from Shiprock. Throughout most of the Utah portion of the route, there was no real road near the line, just a pair of wheel tracks. There were places where it was impossible to get within a quarter mile of the line with a truck. The original builders used horses in the rough terrain, and with close to half century of erosion and neglect, any trails that remained were rough.

I almost always worked toll patrol alone. That meant I always had to be conscious of the fact that if anything went seriously wrong, I was a long way away from anyone who could help. In fact, communication was always a problem. I relied heavily on the radio. Unfortunately, when I was more than thirty or forty miles into Utah, I was out of range of Farmington. From there on, I had to find a big hill and try to contact Monticello, Utah. That usually worked. Trying to talk on the telephone line was often more bother than it was worth, since it was a carrier setup, and the ordinary telephone handset would not work on a carrier. A carrier is an electronic device that makes it possible to carry several conversations on the same wire. I had the option of stopping at Shiprock and patching around the carrier, effectively converting the line to a regular telephone arrangement, but that was not a reliable procedure. Even if the section between my location and the Farmington testboard was clear, Farmington was far away, and with all that resistance and no amplification, we could not hear each other anyway. I had a carrier box that theoretically I could connect and talk on the carrier if it was still operating, but I never had much luck with it.

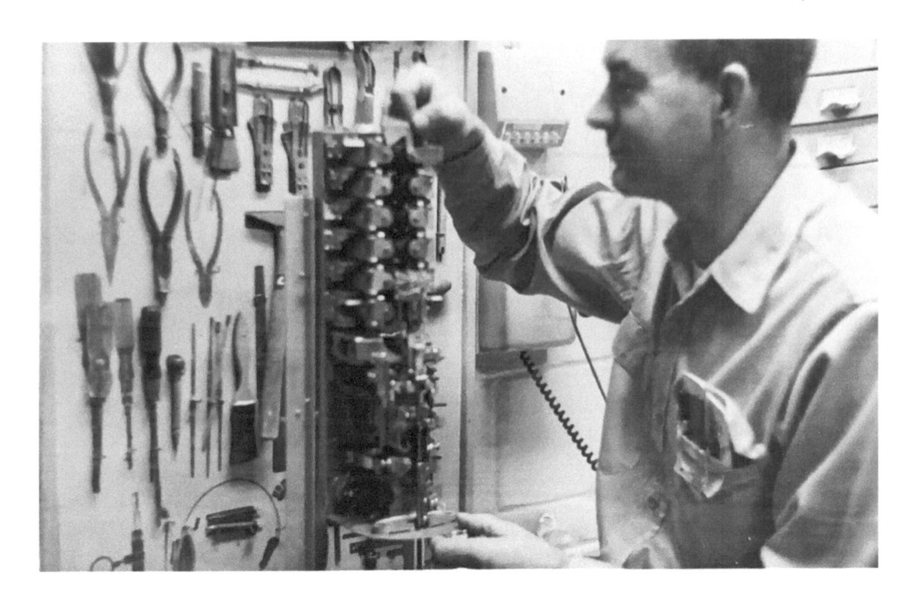

One of my most vivid memories is of the time; I was caught out there in a blizzard. It was a cold gray day when I started out early in the morning, and it snowed all day. The trouble was a long way out. I would drive a while, then stop and cut the line to see if the problem was still beyond me. In the late afternoon the wind came up. It was obvious that it was time to head for home, even though I hadn't found the trouble. I called Monticello on the radio, and told the operator to relay the message to Farmington toll testboard that I was giving up and coming in. My main gas tank was getting low. The next five hours were bad. I was just grinding along, hoping that I could see the trail, and trying to remember where the forks were so that I wouldn't take a wrong turn. Of course, there was no one else out there. I used what gas was left in the main tank and went through the gas in the auxiliary tank. After stopping and pouring in the ten gallons in the jeep cans we always carried for emergencies, I finally made it to the McElmo Canyon road that intersects the highway north of the Four Corners. My gas gauge showed empty by the time I reached the highway. It was 10:00 P.M. I knew the nearest place I could get any gas was Tees Nos Pas, so I headed for the trading post. I must have been running on fumes, but I made it. The man who operated the trading post had gone to bed, but when I pounded on the door of his trailer, he came to the door. When he saw the telephone truck and decided I was OK, he got dressed and unlocked the gas pump, so I could fill up. I was very thankful that I made it home that night.

In 1963, some people were transferred, and I found myself on the bottom of the seniority list. I was assigned to the very job where I started, working in the warehouse. After about two weeks there, I was filling up one of the trucks, when my boss came out to talk to me. He said that he had heard that I had central office experience. I told him yes, that was true; I had been exposed to step-by-step switching when I was in the Army. I was aware that I knew just enough about it to make me dangerous, but I didn't tell him that.

As a result, I was transferred to Aztec immediately as a central office repairman, a top-level craft job. I loved the job, and before long, I got very good at it. Those were two very good years, as far as work was concerned. I was the only person working in the switchroom. I also took care of the little community dial office in Bloomfield.

In 1963 we bought a new Ford, the first brand new car I had ever owned in my life. I had an old 1949 Chevy pickup; actually, a retired telephone truck that I had bought about the time Arlene started the kindergarten. We sold the 1955 Ford that had served us well both on the farm, and during the big move to Farmington.

During 1964, it became obvious that the declining economy was forcing a lot of changes. One Friday afternoon, I got a call to report to the plant office in Farmington. This was very unusual. Vic (Ozell) Roberts was waiting there too. Before long, we got the word that one of us would have to take a transfer to Lordsburg, New Mexico. Because we were so close in seniority, almost the same, they offered it to both of us and left it up to us to decide who would take the transfer. They left us alone for a few minutes to talk it over, and Ozell decided that he would take it. He and I had worked together quite a bit and had gotten to be good friends. I had met his wife Nancy but didn't know her very well at that time. I knew that it wouldn't be long until I was transferred, too.

31

Las Cruces, New Mexico

I got the news at the end of December 1964. I was transferred on very short notice. In fact, I was notified on Friday afternoon that I would have Monday for travel time and would report for work in Socorro on Tuesday. However, the transfer included the very unusual condition that I was to be a roving central office repairman working all over western New Mexico until a backlog of repairs in small community dial offices was completed. After this interim period, I was to be transferred to Las Cruces.

On January 2, 1965, I left for Socorro where for over two months I made my home base while I overhauled the switching equipment, first at New Mexico School of Mines in Socorro, then the little towns of Magdalena, Datil, and Quemado. I had a company truck and lived out of a suitcase, staying in motels. During that time, I hardly got home at all, and Arlene was left to take care of the kids, run the kindergarten, and prepare to move.

When my work in the Socorro area was done, I went back to Farmington to get my old truck and drove to Las Cruces. It didn't take long to get acquainted with the guys I worked with, and I found one friend--Vic Roberts. At work he went by his first name, Victor, but family and close friends knew him by his middle name, Ozell, to distinguish him from his father, Vic. He had gotten very sick while he was in Lordsburg. In fact, he nearly died from polycystic kidney disease. While that was the first time it was diagnosed, he suffered from it the rest of his life, and it eventually killed him over thirty years later. While he made a good recovery from that first attack of the disease, doctors advised him to avoid hard physical work. Because of that limitation, the company did not want him to work outside after that, so he was transferred to Las Cruces and worked in the business office. He never allowed the disease to keep him from living a normal life, until a few years before his death when it became impossible to overcome the handicap.

Ozell and his wife Nancy were very good to me during this transition period. Soon they were like family to us. I will have much more about them later.

Soon after, Arlene came down for a house-hunting trip. I had done some scouting while I was living in a motel, and we soon decided on a house on Laurel Street. Selling the house in Farmington was almost out of the question. There was such a glut of houses on the market there that it was hard to give a house away, let alone sell it. Arlene was able to find a good renter, so we kept it. I made a trip back to Farmington, loaded up a mattress and some bedding, and hauled it to Las Cruces where I stored the stuff in Ozell's garage for a little while until I closed on the house. The company was putting pressure on me to get out of the motel, so as soon as I got possession of the house, I moved my mattress into the house and started sleeping there.

Meanwhile, Arlene was coming to the end of a successful year in the kindergarten. The operetta they performed that spring was so good that the parents wanted her to do it again on local TV, but there just wasn't time because she had to pack up and move. When school was out, we moved. I took a week off and drove 400 miles back to Farmington to get ready to move. We hired a moving company and as soon as our stuff was loaded on the van, we made the long trip to Las Cruces. Arlene drove our car while I drove my old pickup. We timed it so that we would be in Las Cruces when the van arrived.

The same day our furniture was unloaded, the very first evening we all spent in the house, surrounded by piles of boxes, we got a phone call from Iowa. My mother was critically ill. There was nothing we could do but put everything on hold, pile the whole family, including our dog Boots, into the car and head for Iowa. We started out on the 1500-mile trip at 3:30 the next morning after working most of the night. After a few days there my mother seemed to be better, so we made the 1500-mile journey back to Las Cruces. Unfortunately, it was only about a week later when we got the word that my mother had died, so we were on the road again. Somehow, we managed to get unpacked and settled in our new home despite all the problems.

When we moved from Farmington to Las Cruces, Arlene moved all her classroom materials, and wasted no time setting up Cinderella Kindergarten in the new location. She rented a room in the University Methodist Church that was big enough to handle 26 kids in each session. It was a very good arrangement. Not only was there not a kindergarten in the public school, but the school district also leased the other classrooms in the same building for elementary grades. As far as the kids were concerned, it was almost like going to public school because there was a first-grade room right across the hall.

Of course, they could not share playgrounds. Arlene bought her own playground equipment. There were a few downsides to the arrangement. The church used the room for Sunday school, which forced us into the routine of doing the weekly cleaning on Sunday afternoon. The two worst problems were the fact that the church allowed the Boy Scouts to meet there also, and they invariably left the room in a big mess. The other problem was that older kids used and abused the playground equipment when school was not in session. I had to do quite a lot of repair work, because the equipment was never intended to hold kids who were old enough to attend junior high or high school.

Almost from the beginning the kindergarten ran of capacity, one class in the morning, the other in the afternoon. That made a total of 52 kids. There was never any problem in collecting the fees, and the parents were very supportive. A lot of the parents were connected with the university either as students or faculty. The operettas really went over big. We had capacity crowds for every performance. The parents really did a beautiful job on costumes, and the church allowed us to build some elaborate stage sets. The costume I remember the best was a shiny red apple worn by a little girl, with one arm concealed and the other clothed in a bright green "worm." It was a sturdy costume. During the performance the little girl fell and rolled off the stage, which fortunately was only eight inches high. She was not hurt, and the costume was undamaged. Her father picked her up, set her back on her feet, and she went on and spoke her part perfectly as if nothing had happened.

Shortly after I got to Las Cruces, the local union had an election. Even before I had met very many people, I was asked if I would be a candidate for local president. I thought that it wouldn't make any difference if I ran because nobody knew me, and I wouldn't stand a chance of being elected. I knew a little bit about the workings of the union because I had been a steward in Farmington. I accepted the nomination. That was a big mistake. I won the election by a big majority, entirely because the incumbent president was so bad that the members would vote for anybody else but him. If I had known what was involved, I never would have considered the job. It seriously affected our family life as well as my job for the next two years. It was almost like having two jobs. Eight hours a day, (at least) I worked for Mountain Bell. After hours I worked for the union.

Our phone rang at all hours of the night. Arlene answered most of those calls, which were likely to come at any time, even at two in the morning. An uninterrupted night's sleep was a rarity because I was on 24-hour call with Mountain Bell as well. Regrettably, I had very little time to attend the kid's school activities, because I was often somewhere else on union business. It was an unpaid position except that I was reimbursed for travel and out of pocket expenses. I kept good records on mileage because car expense was my main expenditure. For that reason, the mileage is burned into my memory. In the two years I was president, I drove eighteen thousand miles on union business.

The local territory covered about a quarter of New Mexico, so it was not feasible to have just one monthly meeting. I held meetings in Las Cruces, Deming, Silver City and Alamogordo. I often had to go to Albuquerque. The job required me to attend training sessions in Pueblo, Colorado, and Denver as well as the national convention in Kansas City.

Every now and then, I had to go to some other town for a grievance hearing as well. The unions contract provided that any grievance procedure should be held on company time. Some of the things I had to do were satisfying, but some I found myself wearing several different hats. Sometimes it was a legalistic role, explaining or haggling over the interpretation of the contract. In most instances I acted as a negotiator. Often, I found myself acting as a psychologist or sometimes a detective. According to the votes, only a handful of people in Las Cruces thought I wasn't a suitable union president, but I could live with that. I went above and beyond the assignment many times, trying to achieve what I perceived to be the best outcome for the union members regardless of the ranting of my opponents.

My regular job in Las Cruces was interesting and demanding as well. For a while I was assigned as a PBX repairman at New Mexico State University. Western Electric was installing a new step-by-step dial office to serve the whole Campus. I wrote the cross-connect specifications that the installers used to tie all the equipment together. That job took several months. After the new office was cut into service, I was reassigned to work at the Apollo Site at the White Sands Missile Range. I applied for a security clearance soon after I arrived in Las Cruces. Processing a security application takes quite a long time. I could not go to work at the Apollo site full time until my clearance was granted, which fortunately happened soon after the NMSU job was completed.

NASA was testing the lunar landing module, the prototype of the vehicle that landed on the moon. While Mountain Bell crews routinely worked at the site, their access was severely limited. I was the only Mountain Bell employee stationed at Las Cruces at the time that had a security clearance high enough to go into all areas and work on any equipment we had there. Even my boss could not go into many of the areas where I worked. I enjoyed my work there and learned a great deal.

Computer science was just emerging from its infancy. We had only one computer at Apollo, no programmers at all, and our computer was not used for much of anything except assembling weather data, which we sent to NASA at Houston every day. Communication between our machine and Houston was one of my biggest headaches. I spent a great deal of my time fine-tuning the facilities to make the system more reliable, but despite everything the transmission often turned the data into garbage. We used the same technology as a Teletype network to transmit the data. Even at that time Teletype technology was becoming obsolete. The only provision for error detection was a simple parity check, and there was no mechanism for correction at all. The electrical engineer who ran the computer had a whole shelf full of books on how to program the machine, but he did not know how, and was not particularly interested in learning. He invited me to study the IBM manuals, which I attempted to do, but didn't get far. For one thing I simply didn't have time.

Soon after we got settled in Las Cruces, Arlene got well acquainted with Nancy Roberts. They lived quite close to us. All our family was far away, so we started having our holiday dinners together with the Roberts family. That started a tradition that has lasted a lifetime. Nancy and Arlene pretended they were sisters to have visiting privileges whenever one of them had to go to the hospital. Before long, our kids began referring to them as their aunt and uncle, so in effect we adopted an extended family. Nancy was Arlene's substitute teacher at the kindergarten.

Like sisters, Arlene and Nancy Roberts

Before we moved, David had a paper route in Farmington, delivering papers with his bike. He took it very seriously and made spending money. He got a route in Las Cruces that was longer and more demanding, as well as giving him a pretty good income for a kid. The Sunday papers were big and heavy, so I usually ran the route with my pickup on Sunday morning. He stood in the back and threw the papers as I drove. Once I made a U-turn a little too fast and threw him off the truck! Luckily, he was not badly hurt, just a little road rash.

David was very interested in music. He had gotten a saxophone when we were in Farmington, and before long was so proficient that he was ready for a better instrument. With his paper route money and a little help from us, he bought a very good Selmer sax, which he has kept and played ever since.

Music became the focus of much of their social activity. All three of the kids were good students and got good grades. We were a little disappointed with Cheryl's teacher, but she liked school and apparently it was not hard for her to keep up with schoolwork and get good grades later in Colorado.

David built another science project that won first place in Las Cruces that qualified him to take it to Soccorro and enter it in the state science fair. When we saw the projects on display, we soon realized that students whose fathers worked in the labs in Albuquerque and Los Alamos made most of the other top projects. They were very advanced, showing that the parents had a lot of input. Anyway, it was a learning experience, and we were proud of David's effort even if he didn't win first prize.

One of the more unusual things that David and I did together grew out of his intense interest in science. I worked with electronics all the time but felt that I could use some more education. When I started talking about taking an adult education class in electronics at New Mexico State, David wanted to take it too. Of course, he was still in junior high, but I knew he was ready for it, so we talked to the instructor about admitting him to the class. He was surprised but cooperative, so Dave and I went to night school together. I found the work easy, for much of it was review for me. Dave soaked it up like a sponge. When it came time for the final test, guess who got the highest grade in the class--David! He did not get any credits, but the learning experience was worthwhile anyway.

I had very little time for any social activity, but despite that, I started singing barbershop style with the Border Chorders of El Paso, Texas. I always carpooled with another guy to go to practice in El Paso once a week, but that was the extent of my involvement at that time.

Sometime during this period, probably in 1966, the company invited certain individuals throughout the company to take a programming aptitude test. Both Ozell and I took it. Both of us had also gone through the assessment session, which qualified us as candidates for management positions. He was immediately accepted and transferred to Denver for training as a programmer. His promotion did not surprise me in the least, because I was already convinced, he was one of the smartest guys I knew. For some time after that, I heard nothing to indicate whether I passed the test or not, and completely forgot about it.

On a Friday afternoon in the late summer of 1967, I had just gotten home from work when I got a phone call. It was my boss. He informed me that I was being offered a promotion and transfer to Denver for training as a programmer if I wanted it. He explained that I would have to take a cut in pay, because I would become a salaried employee and lose the abundance of overtime that I had been getting. The company would pay our moving expense and take care of selling our house if I chose to go. However, I had to make up my mind right away. They had already scheduled a conference call for 9:00 the next morning to arrange the details. Arlene and I talked it over for a little while, and I called back and told him I would take it. Of course, I still had until 9:00 A. M. the next day to confirm my decision. It was a harder decision for Arlene than it was for me because her kindergarten business was really going well so that she was making at least as much money as I was, if not more. It was a gamble that eventually I would be able to earn a high enough salary to make up for the temporary loss of income. Of course, I was considering that fact that I was at the top of the pay scale for a non-management employee, so my only possibility of making more money was to go into management.

At the time that I decided to take the transfer, both David and Paul were in a band camp in Portales, New Mexico. We arranged to make a house-hunting trip to Denver, leaving the following weekend. When we picked up the boys at the campus of Eastern New Mexico University, we broke the news to them that we were going to Denver. It must have been a shock to them, but they took the news very well. We had bought a new Chrysler in Las Cruces, so we had three vehicles, and only two drivers. We drove both our Ford and our Chrysler to Denver and left the Ford with Nancy and Ozell until we made the move. We made a very fast tour of available houses, and soon decided on a house on Sylvia Drive in Northglenn. Nancy and Ozell were living in Northglenn, about three miles from our new home.

Back in Las Cruces we had to make a lot of arrangements in a very short time. Arlene was all prepared to start a new school year. Then something completely unexpected happened-- she had a miscarriage. With all the pressure to get ready to move, it made things a lot harder for her. She let someone else take over the kindergarten and got nothing whatsoever for it, which was a shame. I resigned my union job, thankful to get out from under the responsibility. Of course, I was not eligible to be a union member any more as soon as I got my new job title as a management employee. My elected term would have expired in four months. I did what training I could to get a new guy ready to take over at Apollo, but I left with the feeling that it was not an orderly turnover. I was quite aware that the man who took over was poorly prepared for what I had been doing and underestimated the scope and difficulty of the job. However, I had a whole new set of responsibilities to assume. As far as I was concerned, I was through with it, and would not worry about it anymore.

I know that Arlene liked Las Cruces, while David thought it was OK and Paul loved it. He and the boy next door, Jerry Denney, had become best friends, and had a lot of fun together. I think that Cheryl was happy there, but she drew a rather lazy teacher for 5th grade, and really didn't get the quality of schooling she had experienced before. I was glad to get out of Las Cruces. I must admit that the union position forced me to learn a great deal about interaction with other people, but I also had to learn to live with a strong element of politics that I hated.

My old truck that I brought from Farmington had developed a terminal illness on a business trip to Albuquerque about a year before. I had bought it very cheap when I first got it and got good service from it for a lot of years. I sold it for junk price in Albuquerque and bought a white 1962 Chevy pickup while I was there. The '62 was a good truck, but it had been used hard before I bought it.

The move to Denver was hard work for me, but it was that and a painful ordeal as well for Arlene. She did not have time to really recover from the miscarriage. After we got our furniture loaded on the van, we made the long drive to Denver again. Arlene drove the Chrysler, and I drove my truck.

The day we left Las Cruces we started a little later than we would have liked. We managed to make it to Trinidad. Of course, we should have stopped earlier. By the time we got there, Arlene was so exhausted and hurting so much she couldn't go on, and every good motel we tried was full. We ended up in a so-called motel that was so bad, that we didn't even dare open our suitcases. That was one of the worst places we ever stayed while traveling.

32

Denver and Northglenn, Colorado

We arrived in Denver on Labor Day weekend, September 1, 1967. When we first came, we moved into a motel where we stayed for a month. We soon got possession of the house on Sylvia Drive, but Arlene wanted to clean and redecorate before we moved in. The company paid for the motel, so we took advantage of the arrangement.

The kids started school immediately. The schools, especially the high school, were overcrowded so we had to learn to live with split sessions. Each child was in a different school, and the hours were different in each one. It was a hard adjustment for the kids, and Arlene had to assume a much bigger role as the family taxi driver, just to take the kids to and from school. School was more stressful for the whole family than it had been before, for a good many reasons. Of course, some of the strain was simply the inevitable difficulty of making transitions from elementary to junior high to high school. Some of it was the overcrowding of the schools. Another factor was getting acquainted and making new friends. We were making a big change that was considerably more difficult than the move from Farmington to Las Cruces had been. Most of the time, though, everything worked out all right and we did not regret making the move. All the kids did well in school and were honor students. Cheryl made the honor role in 6th grade, which was encouraging, because at first we were afraid that her 5th grade in the Las Cruces school was not up to the standards she needed to make a good transition. Before long, the kids had a new circle of friends and felt at home in our new community

We started looking for a church right away. One of the first churches we visited was the Lutheran Church of Hope in Broomfield. We liked it and joined almost immediately. It was a very small congregation, mostly made up of families like us who had moved from Iowa, Minnesota, Nebraska, North Dakota, and South Dakota. A lot of them were Scandinavians, too. We soon became involved in church activities. All our kids were confirmed in that church. Over the years Arlene served as Sunday school teacher, Sunday school superintendent and teacher trainer, and volunteered to do numerous other jobs. Both of us helped with the altar guild. I taught a Sunday school class for a while and taught a confirmation class for a year. I soon joined the church choir and when Arlene was able to turn over some of her other jobs to younger people, she joined it too.

Meanwhile, I was totally immersed in programming school. At that time, it was a Mountain Bell enterprise, conducted in a Mountain Bell building, but taught by IBM personnel. I firmly believe that there was a certain amount of snobbery involved. The IBM folk felt that they were smarter than telephone company people and were somewhat condescending in the way that they approached teaching. This was not necessarily a personal attitude of the instructors; it was a manifestation of the IBM company subculture and was instilled into their people by IBM management throughout their organization. I had a tough time in the school. I was very scared of being flunked out of the training probably with good reason. I remember imposing on Ozell at one point to try to get past some point where I was stuck. He gave me very straightforward answers, which cleared up some things that had remained a complete mystery to me when the same things came up in class. In short, I found I could learn more from him in a half-hour than I could in a week of class. I will never know how close I came to flunking out, but in any case, I did make it through the course and graduate.

Learning did not end with school. That was just the beginning. The job was not only a hard never-ending series of tasks; it was a constant search for solutions. Many problems had been solved before, so with some diligence one could find the code and copy or paraphrase it, but for an unbelievable number of applications, there was no previous work to fall back on. In most cases, we were converting manual tasks to a machine operation. Methods that had been evolved with generations of human effort were frequently impossible or hopelessly expensive to duplicate on the machines we had to work with. Those computers were huge. Compared with the computers we use now, they had very little processing power, but compared with the devices that preceded them, they were nothing short of miraculous.

Punch card machines were the evolutionary predecessors of computers, and in our daily work we had elements of both. The only keyboard that could communicate with the computer directly was an electric typewriter located on the computer operator's console, not available to the programmer at all. There was no screen, only commands typed on paper by the operator and responses typed on the same paper by the computer. Operating the computer was a completely different skill than programming, and in theory the programmer never saw the computer. In practice, we often performed both specialties for the simple reason that we worked whenever necessary, 24 hours a day seven days a week. If there was no computer operator on duty, we turned on the lights, powered up the machines, and ran our own programs.

As programmers we were never in direct communication with the computer. We wrote the code in pencil in a rigidly structured format on a sheet of paper. The only way to transform this handwritten code into a form that the computer could read was to type it on the keyboard of a keypunch machine. The keypunch produced a punched card for every line of code we had written. This produced a deck of cards that was the executable program. A card reader machine read these cards one by one and fed the instructions into the computer every time the program was executed. Some of these program decks could consist of two thousand cards or more. In fact, some of the toll programs which computed the time and charges for long distance calls were larger than that.

The memory built into those early mainframes was tiny compared to what we have now. In fact, the largest machine we had at the time I started had 16K of memory. The little laptop on which I am writing now has eight thousand times as much! I mention that only to emphasize the technical difficulty we faced in writing programs. Every byte was precious. Therefore, we went to elaborate lengths to save memory and storage space. Processors were slow too, so efficiency was very important. There were no tools available to aid the programmer. All the programs were written in assembly language, which is only one level above the actual binary instructions that the machine executes. Operating systems were in their infancy. In fact, the first operating system ever released for general use had only been available for about two years when I started programming.

We still had the house in Farmington when we moved to Denver, but our good renter had been transferred out of the state, so we had to rent it to someone else. They did not take good care of it, and we soon were paying a lot of repair bills. We were paying a realtor to manage it for us, but he wasn't doing a satisfactory job. Reluctantly we had to let it go. The housing market in Farmington was still very bad, so the best we could do was to sell it to someone who would pay the closing costs and take over the payments. We lost our entire equity.

I worked so many hours those first few years that I had little time left over for anything else. Our family situation changed too. Arlene got pregnant again soon after we moved. Kristen was born in June 1968. The other kids were old enough by then to be a big help. Kristen got plenty of love and attention!

Arlene wanted to spend as much time as she could with the kids, so she decided not to start the kindergarten again. She started teaching kindergarten in a private school in Northglenn when Kristen was a year old. In 1974 kindergarten was offered in the public schools, so the situation was completely different from what she faced in New Mexico. She switched to preschool teaching in an established preschool at the Village Baptist Church. The children were younger of course than those she had worked with previously, but she was comfortable with them and managed to teach them quite a bit anyway. She took a course at an extension of the University of Northern Colorado held at Community College and was certified to be a preschool director in Colorado. However, she never went back into business for herself. She worked at another preschool in Broomfield the last few years before she retired. Altogether, she spent 35 years in the classroom. She also volunteered to work in the library of Malley Elementary School that Kristen attended.

David went through high school at Northglenn High and graduated in 1970. He was always one of the top students in his class. There was never any doubt that he would go into science, and from a very young age he was especially interested in chemistry. Along the way he picked up a lot of knowledge of computers too and was writing programs while he was still in high school. He continued to play his sax and played first chair alto sax in the band.

In the fall of 1970, I got an unexpected phone call that changed my life. The caller introduced himself as Bill Ewing and explained that he was starting a community singing group. He had called some churches, gotten names of people who sang in church choirs, and was recruiting. I had been wishing I had some other activity besides work and going to church, so I agreed to come to a practice. After the first time, I went back week after week, and it became a welcome break from the daily grind. Now, more than 32 years later, I am still singing with the Northland Chorale.

Paul attended Huron Junior High, where he was a very good student and loved playing in the band. He always played woodwinds. He started with the clarinet, but when the director needed someone to play the bass clarinet, he took over that spot in the concert band. It was a very good junior high band. Moving on to high school he played in the concert band, and the marching band that won the state championship year after year. Paul was a good student, but of course he was different from David, and being in his brother's shadow inevitably created some problems for him. Rather than accepting him for what he was, some teachers compared him with David, and one even accused him of copying his brother's work. In fact, he was a very talented writer, a good student in science and math, but not getting the respect for his achievements that David did. He became increasingly unhappy in school, although he always had a circle of friends, particularly in the band.

David graduated from Northglenn High School in 1970 and started at the Colorado School of Mines in the fall. He majored in chemistry, which had always been his primary interest. He also worked for some of the professors there and got a very good education and a lot of practical knowledge from his years there.

Paul was the farmer in our family. He was always intensely interested in horses and livestock in general. Soon after we moved to Northglenn, he became acquainted with some of the old neighbors who still had farmland close to our house. The Patterson acreage, on the southwest comer of 120th and Washington soon became his special place. Mr. and Mrs. Patterson were quite elderly and could not do a lot of physical work. Paul did a lot of little chores for them, and in return they let him have the run of the place. There was a barn some distance from the other buildings, approximately where the Northglenn Post Office is now. When Paul first saw it, old boards, mouse-infested straw bales, a little old machinery, and just plain junk filled it to the rafters. He completely cleaned it out and loaded the junk on my truck. I made two or three trips to the dump to dispose of the stuff; otherwise, he did all the work himself. He put the little homemade tractor to good use dragging stuff out. There was a pasture adjacent to the barn that belonged to Mr. Carlson. Soon afterward Paul and I bought a pair of Black Angus steers from one of the Carlson brothers and put them in the pasture. They were high quality, suitable for 4-H club calves, so they were not cheap. Unfortunately, the pasture fences were beyond fixing so we had to stake the steers out on ropes for a while. I built a feed bunk and fixed up a barrel for hauling water on the truck. Using some junked telephone poles, we built a little pen so the calves did not have to be tied up. Later we built a sturdy fenced yard adjacent to the barn so that the cattle could use the barn as well.

Paul had the use of a horse too. It actually belonged to Mr. Carlson. While the Carlson family was not ready to sell it, they did not have time to ride or look after the horse, so Paul rode it and took care of it. It was a gentle little horse. Paul did not have a saddle, so he rode bareback until he bought a saddle pad. It was usually boarded at a farm a few miles away, but Paul often rode it over to the Patterson place, and kept it there for short periods.

He had a natural ability to handle horses, more than I ever had, even though I worked with horses from the time I was a little kid until I was in my late teens. Paul rented some hayfields around the neighborhood and put up the hay to feed his cattle. A little side note here-- when Cheryl was old enough to get her drivers learning permit, I took her out in the stick shift Ford and let her get behind the wheel. It was immediately obvious that she already knew how to drive and handled the clutch and gearshift as though she already had lots of experience. I said,

"How long have you been driving?"

"About two years."

Paul had taught her how to drive the truck out in the hayfield picking up bales. Having learned driving a four-speed stick shift truck with a load, driving a car was no problem.

Cheryl spent her junior high years at Huron Junior High, and went on to high school at Northglenn, where she continued to be an honor student, and maintained high grades throughout her high school career. She played a sax in the concert band and was a member of the marching band that won many championships.

Paul, Cheryl, David and Kristen
Northglenn, CO, 1970

The old barn on Patterson's place was used for another purpose too. The Northland Chorale was very short of money in the early years of its existence. I was the treasurer and was getting tired of putting off the creditors we owed for the music. Someone thought of the idea of having a barn sale to raise money. We had no calves in the barn at that time. We cleaned up the barn and filled it with donated items and had a sale. We made enough to get the chorale out of debt. In fact, that was the turning point for the chorale. We still had to watch our expenses, but the chorale has never operated in the red again in its 32 years of existence.

When the steers were ready, we had the Eastlake frozen food locker take care of getting them butchered and packaging and freezing the meat. We bought a big home freezer, filled it, and sold the rest.

When Paul figured out what he had spent in buying and feeding the steers, it was clear that he hadn't made any money. We talked it over, and he decided it might be better to buy a cheaper animal even though it wouldn't finish out as well as the Angus. I knew from experience that it often worked out that way, and I suggested that a Holstein steer might be the best bet.

We went to the sale barn, and as luck would have it, there were no Holstein steers at all that day. There was one steer that looked like a Guernsey that he bid on and he got it fairly cheap. We borrowed a horse trailer and hauled it home. Right then and there I realized that we had a skittish critter on our hands, one that would likely always be a problem to handle. I felt a little bad for letting him go ahead and buy the steer but I didn't want to say too much.

The steer was manageable for a while, but then something happened that we never would have imagined. Someone, probably teenage kids, shot and wounded him. He went berserk, broke through the fence, got out in heavy traffic on 120th Avenue and created a traffic problem. When cornered he charged and was obviously dangerous. Arlene, Paul, and Cheryl tried to round him up without success. The Northglenn police tried their hand at it and had no luck at all. They called the Adams County animal control officer who succeeded in roping him and tying him to a horse trailer. He promptly broke the lariat rope and took off again. They tried another rope; but he got away trailing the rope until he lost it. By then I had gotten off work, and Dave and I tried to see what we could do. Finally, he jumped a fence and got out into Stan Carlson's big pasture. We decided to let him stay there overnight, hoping he would settle down.

He didn't settle down. We found him the next morning in a plowed field about a half-mile north of the pasture. We chased him back into the pasture. By this time, I had located a cowboy who said he would rope him for us. The cowboy and his wife arrived with their horse trailer and two horses. They pulled out in the pasture, unloaded the horses, and proceeded to chase the steer at a dead run. They made a perfect head and heel catch on the first try and stretched him out on the ground. They dragged him into the trailer and hauled him back to the barn. By this time, we had barricaded the barn so that he couldn't get out, and we never let him out again until we loaded him into a trailer to go to be butchered. We fed him for a few more weeks but were never able to get in the pen with him. As soon as I climbed up on the top of the gate, he would charge. He acted more like a bad-tempered bull than any steer I ever worked with.

Paul had enough credits to graduate from high school by the end of the first semester of his senior year. He probably would have graduated at that time if we had agreed to let him do so. We wanted him to stay at home until the end of the school year and graduate with the majority of his class. He could take a class in biochemistry, which he liked, and start taking college courses as well. He wanted to graduate and get a job, but we talked him into staying in school. I know he wanted very much to get out of high school, but we felt it would be best for him to stay the extra semester since he was still only 17 years old. His 18th birthday was in May, very close to the end of the school year. He started taking courses in welding and auto mechanics at Metro Community College and continued with the biochemistry class at the high school. He wanted to go into veterinary medicine and there is no doubt he would have made a good veterinarian. He was already accepted at Iowa State University although he could have gone to other schools as well.

There was an incident on a band trip, which in retrospect, we later recognized as the beginning of his downward spiral. Someone tricked him into taking a drug, which was probably LSD. He had a terrible reaction and passed out on the bus on the way home. The band director called 911 and the paramedics met the bus as soon as possible and rushed him to the hospital. The hospital admitted him and kept him overnight. He was apparently okay when he was released, but I know he had flashbacks more than once the following year. He seemed to lose his optimistic outlook permanently at that time.

Unfortunately, we did not pick up on any signs that he was so unhappy that he would think of suicide. He had a girlfriend who was not good for him at all. She was very possessive, chronically unhappy, and probably was quite depressed. Certainly, she made Paul's depression worse. I think he felt trapped because he didn't know how to break off the relationship even if he wanted to go away to school and make a new start.

February 17, 1972 was, and still is, the most terrible day in our lives. I was experiencing severe pressure at work, so I was tired and grouchy when I got home. Paul had a bad day too. I don't remember all the details, but I know he told Arlene that he had rented an apartment with another guy and was going to move out. She told him that she loved him very much and wanted him to stay in his room till he graduated.

He was making plans to go to work for a custom harvester after graduation and follow the wheat harvest. I also wanted him to stay home until he graduated. The part about the harvest run was okay with me although I privately thought he would have to be 18 before he could get the job, although he had already talked to the boss and was sure he could do it. Paul and I each had our say and that's all there was to it. Of course, we had disagreed now and then, but I cannot recall any time that we ever got into a real argument. His normal way of handling any disagreement was to say what he had to say and if the other person disagreed, he would not respond. That did not mean that he was giving in, far from it. He was just like my father in that respect. He let you know how things were and that was the end of it as far as he was concerned. Arlene had a meeting that night at school, so she left. I think he then made some phone calls from his room.

I was sitting in the family room downstairs when he came in and told me that he should move out. I insisted he should stay until he graduated. We didn't agree; we just quit talking and I went to bed. He turned up the radio very loud in his room, which was also something he had never done before.

When Arlene came home from her meeting, she went down to Paul's room to check on him. I heard her screaming, jumped out of bed, and ran down to his room. He was lying dead on the floor, his .22 rifle beside him. He had shot himself in the head.

We buried him in the Elmwood cemetery in Brighton, Colorado. We chose that cemetery because it was in more of a rural community than the other ones nearby. Also, Paul liked Brighton and made many trips over there with his little Datsun pickup. He was buried in a single lot. The cemetery has since filled in, so there is no possibility that we will be buried anywhere close to him.

There were three deaths in the family within six months in 1971 and 1972. The first was Arlene's dad, Mandius Hanson. The next was Paul, and the last was Arlene's mother, Johanna, who came to stay with us for a while after Paul's death and helped Arlene get through that terrible time.

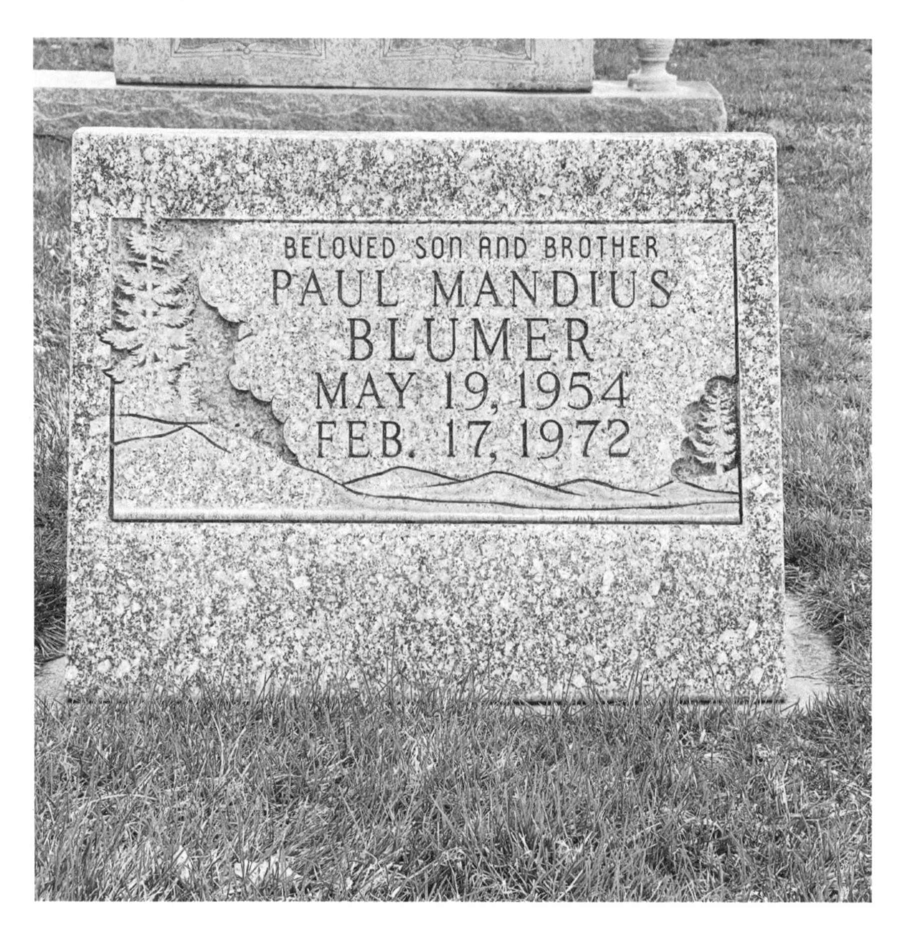

33

Scandinavia

Arlene and me center, surrounded by good friends

We had been planning to make a trip to Norway for some time before all this happened. The original plan was for Mandius, Johanna, Arlene, David, Paul, Cheryl, and me to go together. After Mandius died, Johanna was still determined to go, and we had already bought the tickets. Before the departure date, Johanna passed away as well. Of course, we were still grieving for Paul, as well as for Mandius and Johanna, but we decided to go ahead anyway. Arlene's brother Johnny decided to go with us.

The overseas flight was a charter out of Minneapolis with the Nordman's Forbundet, a group of Norwegians. They were a very friendly group, and we enjoyed the trip. Once in Oslo, we were on our own. We managed to find a nice place to stay while we rested from the trip and explored Oslo. Our destination was Mandius' homeport, Haugesund, in the fjord country on the west coast of Norway.

We took the train across Norway to Bergen, enjoying a lot of fine scenery on the way. Of course, everything was new to us, but for novice travelers we did well. Usually, we could find someone who could speak English, and Arlene could understand a lot of Norwegian although she soon discovered that the language she had learned from her dad and mother was obsolete, more like Swedish than the modern Norwegian. In fact, the Norwegians make a distinction between "new Norwegian" and "old Norwegian".

The next leg of our trip was fun, too. We boarded the hydrofoil that made a regular run from Bergen to Stavanger every day, with a stop of Haugesund. None of us had ever been on one of those boats before, and we were amazed at how fast it was. The foils from which the craft gets its name are like underwater wings. At rest, the hull of the boat is down in the water like an ordinary boat, with the foils deep in the water, but as it gathers speed the hull lifts out of the water, leaving only the propellers submerged and the foils skim along just under the surface. The craft cruised at over 40 knots--about 50 miles an hour.

There were several people who got off the boat at Haugesund, but Arlene's relatives who had come to meet us picked us out of the crowd immediately.

Our host and hostess were Olav and Margit Larsen. Margit is Arlene's first cousin. They showed us wonderful hospitality. We soon learned that when they take a period off from work, they call that their holiday, while would refer to it as vacation. We came at the time when most of the people in the country were on their holiday. Most of the people in the country, except for essential workers, take their holiday at the same time.

Olav was a partner and service manager at the largest Ford dealership on the west coast of Norway. He took us on a tour of their shop, which was really an auto rebuilding plant. It was a spotless, wonderfully efficient plant where cars were completely rebuilt, rolling off the assembly line as good as new. It was also a teaching facility participating in a government program to train young mechanics. On the second day we were there, Olav took David and me to the lot where they stored their cars. He walked down the line to a brand-new red German Ford and handed David the keys. That was our car for the rest of our stay.

With Margit and Olav, their four kids, and our whole party we went on a driving and hiking tour of Norway's highlands. We saw a lot of fjords, too. We stayed in camping huts at night where for a few cents we could roll out our bedrolls and get a good night's sleep. The high spot of the trip was hiking in the Hardanger Vidda, which although it is a little below the Arctic Circle, has an arctic climate because of its altitude. It is tundra. No trees grow there, only reindeer moss and a few creeping bushes that grow no higher than the moss. Walking in the moss is deceptive. As you look over it, what you see is a smooth light green expanse. When you walk in it, you find yourself in a spongy blanket 18 inches thick where you sink into ankle deep water with almost every step. Furthermore, the moss conceals everything underneath, even holes between the invisible rocks. A couple of the girls stepped into holes and found themselves waist deep in icy water. We were gathering berries and got a pretty good harvest. They were delicious. After we got back to Olav and Margit's place, Margit made some very tasty desserts with them.

We went fishing, too. One of Olav's friends took us out in the ocean in his little boat and we brought home a nice bunch of mackerel. I didn't catch any of them. Arlene snagged a big fish that almost pulled her out of the boat, but even with help from the men, the fish got away.

After the visit with Olav and Margit and her other cousin Solveig and the aunts and uncles, we left for Oslo again. This time we traveled by bus to a town where we could catch a different train back to Oslo. Again, the scenery was wonderful.

We made another trip to Scandinavia in 1979. Arlene, Kristen, and I went with Wayne and Ann Peterson and joined a tour group in Oslo. We really enjoyed the bus tour. Of course, we were familiar with some places in Norway, but having the tour guide was a great experience because he told us many interesting things about the places we were visiting. The other people on the tour included a group from Alexandria, MN, who had arranged an audience with the King of Sweden. We were not cleared with the Swedish security, so we did not attend the visit although the people who did told us later that it would have been all right anyway. The tour started in Oslo, visited several places in Norway, and then crossed over into Sweden, then finally, after an extensive tour of Sweden, crossed on a ferry to Denmark. We had become good friends with some of the other people on the tour by the time it ended in Copenhagen. It was a great experience.

We then went to Norway on our own to visit the relatives for a few days. The trip from Copenhagen to Norway was an ordeal, partly because I did not understand that buying a ticket on the train did not include reserving a seat. As a result, we had to stand all the way across Denmark, except when some other passengers were kind enough to trade off and let Arlene and Kristen sit for a while. We did not get a chance to eat either. Kristen was not feeling well by the time we boarded the ferry to cross over to Kristiansand, and the water was extremely rough, so she got very seasick. The poor kid didn't feel well for most of the time we were in Norway. We visited with the relatives but didn't do much else during the week we were there.

The high point of the visit was an overnight stay on the island of Finay where Olav and Margit have a house that has been in his family for a long time. The house was about 250 years old at that time. They had partially restored it at the time we were there. It has an interesting history. For a good part of its life, probably more than a century, it served as the only inn on the island. One room was used as a store that was kept in business well into the twentieth century. The house has a place in Norwegian history as well. It was the home and headquarters of Cleng Peerson, who organized the first group emigration of Norwegians to America. I am not sure of the date, but my guess is that the first shipload of immigrants came over in the 1870's. I could not get into the room where the travelers had stayed in the inn but peeked through the nailed-up door and saw the old bed frames, with remnants of the rope that once supported straw mattresses, lined up on both sides of the big room.

The furniture that we used was not as old as the house, but very old nevertheless, mostly probably 100 to 150 years old. We slept upstairs in a room that was accessed by a ladder. Arlene and I first tried a bed that was like those we had seen in museums, a very short, narrow crib-like arrangement. Even nested together like two spoons we could not stand being crammed into the bed very long, so I soon traded with Kristen who had a modern army cot and got some sleep.

Our return trip home was entirely by air, leaving from Haugesund to Oslo, then a flight from Oslo to Copenhagen, then Copenhagen to Chicago, and finally Chicago to Denver.

34

Home Again

David, Me, Cheryl, Kristen, Arlene

Back home, we had to continue adjusting to living without Paul. As I have told many people over the years, you never get over losing a child. You just get used to it. I was glad I had a good job where I could keep myself occupied, and not have too much time to brood about his suicide. I learned what a wonderful thing it was to have the support of the people in the church, the neighborhood, and the Northland

Chorale. I became very close friends with the people in the Chorale. Over the years, it has been almost like an extended family to me. Nancy and Ozell were a big help at that time also.

I have many good memories of the semi-annual Chorale shows. We always put on at least four performances of each show and many of them went six or seven. For several years, almost every performance was sold out.

I have sung in every show the Chorale has ever staged except for six. One was performed when I was temporarily working in California, and the other five were put on during the years I was working in New Jersey. Of the shows I have been in, I have never missed a performance unless I was out of town, and that has only happened on two weekends in all that time-- a total of three performances.

Eventually, the voters of the Denver metro area approved the formation of the Cultural Facilities District and the Chorale began receiving a subsidy from the taxpayers. That has been both good and bad. The good part is that we have had a lot of money to work with. The downside is that there is a lot of competition now with new groups that have started so it is harder to attract singers and harder to sell tickets to our performances as well.

We had started a tradition of having our holiday celebrations with Nancy and Ozell and the kids when we were in Las Cruces and continued to do so in Northglenn. Over almost four decades there have been relatively few years when we missed having Thanksgiving and Christmas dinners together. Of course, there were years when we lived far apart, but when we all finally returned to our neighborhood, we kept up the tradition even though some of our loved ones are gone and others have been added.

David graduated from Colorado School of Mines in 1974 and went on to the University of Illinois in Champagne-Urbana. He finished his resident work there and moved to California for his first big job with Occidental Petroleum in 1979.

Cheryl graduated from Northglenn High School in 1974 and went to New Mexico State University in Las Cruces that fall. She and Steve

Oathout were married in 1976, and she moved to Tucson with him and finished her college years at the University of Arizona. We really didn't want her to get married before she finished college, but after our experience with Paul we were afraid to say so. We regretted that later. Cheryl graduated in 1979, just before her oldest boy, David, was born. Even with the additional responsibilities of marriage and pregnancy, she maintained a high grade point average.

Sometime in the mid-70's I began singing barbershop again and was a member of the Denver Mile Hi chorus for eight years. We entered the chorus competition every year. At the time I was a member, there were about 750 choruses entered in the first contest each year. The top sixteen groups go to the international contest and convention each year. While I was a member, we made it into that select group six times. I have memories of singing to big crowds, especially in Cincinnati, St. Louis, Seattle, and Salt Lake City. Our best ranking was seventh. We were proud of our record, because the competition is tough when you get that close to the international championship.

This is to certify that

JAMES A BLUMER

has been accepted as a member in good standing of the

DENVER *chapter of the*

Society for the Preservation and Encouragement of Barber Shop Quartet Singing in America

(An incorporated not-for-profit educational and charitable Society Founded in the State of Oklahoma)

He is hereby granted all Rights and Privileges in accordance with the By-Laws of his Chapter and of the Society, and He is entitled to Harmonize at any time, day or night, subject only to the Code of Ethics and other rules and regulations of the Society and conforming always to the applicable laws pertaining to the preservation of the public peace.

In Witness Hereof, *this Certificate has been signed and presented.*

Barrie Best
EXECUTIVE DIRECTOR

CHAPTER SECRETARY

August 15, 1976
DATE

35

The Philippines

I went to Manila, Philippines, in January 1980 on a business trip for Mountain Bell. In a great many respects, I feel that this period was the peak of my career with Mountain Bell. Although I was involved in many conversions of records from a manual system to computer, this was the biggest. I was one of the managers assigned with the responsibility of implementing the conversion of assignment records of all the facilities owned by the company. That included every piece of central office equipment, every pair of wires in every cable, every telephone number and every piece of company owned equipment on customer premises in our company area.

These records had been kept as handwritten entries in cable books and line cards since the founding of the company. They were written in pencil so that they could be erased and written over as assignments changed. The heavy pages were used until repeated erasures wore through the paper. Then they were copied by hand onto fresh pages. Our job was to create an enormous computer, database and load all this information into it.

The first major task was to convert the paper records into a form that the computer could read. The job of microfilming all the records and typing the data into magnetic tape was so enormous that the possibility of having our own employees do it was never seriously considered. There was only one company in the United Sates that would even consider bidding on the job. Their bid was so high that the higher management of Mountain Bell decided that we would have to go overseas to get the job done at a price we could afford.

This was the point where I entered the picture. I wrote the technical specifications that eventually were included in the contract. I participated in the discussions with the president and the general manager of Saztec International, which was awarded the contract. Saztec was an Australian company that had facilities in Manila and Singapore capable of doing the data entry work we wanted.

The first attempt to load the database with tapes we received from Manila failed. Many of the problems were caused by errors in our loading specifications. Of course, I had to accept my share of the blame for that although in many of those instances the data from which I wrote the specs was incomplete or wrong. Also, I was the manager of the programming group that wrote the definitions and programs from those specifications. We fixed those program errors relatively quickly. My programmers, analysts and I worked some unbelievably long hours, but we got the job done. Teaching the people in Manila how to interpret our instructions was a tougher problem. We first tried to work things out by long distance, but it soon became obvious that we weren't getting much done that way.

Someone in the executive office suite decided that the company would have to send someone to Manila to straighten things out. Jim Schmidt from the engineering department was the best-qualified cable records expert, and I knew as much as anybody about the computer side of the job, so the two of us were sent to Manila.

It was a long, tiring ride--27 hours, including layovers from the time we left Denver till we arrived in Manila. Once there, the president of Saztec, Alan Frazer, gave us the VIP treatment, put us up at one of the best hotels in town, and assigned each of us an office in the high-rise building at 221 Buendia Ave. It is called the Great Pacific Life building. We worked in the offices of Pacific Data Corporation, which was the subcontractor for Saztec on the job. My office was next door to that of

Emmanuel (Manny) Cu who was the general manager of Pacific Data. We were there only a month, but it was a memorable month. I worked at least twelve hours most days, quite a few times fifteen or sixteen hours, and during the whole time took only one whole day and another half day off. It was worth it though. We solved a lot of problems and cleared up a lot of misunderstandings.

With little free time, I didn't get much sightseeing done, but certainly enjoyed what I did. One afternoon a taxi driver took me to see a lot of the sights. He was a good tour guide too and told me a lot of interesting things about the city. The most memorable, if more than a little bit disturbing was the old Spanish powder magazine that was used as a prison by the Japanese in World War II. It is a low, massive stone bunker with no windows and only one door. POWs were thrown in on top of those who had already died and left to perish. When the Americans entered the city after recapturing it from the Japanese, they removed the bodies of 550 POWs from the building. There is a monument in front if it now commemorating those who died.

The taxi driver also took me to see the poorest sections of Manila (the squatter shacks on the mudflats along the coast) and the richest (the presidential palace and Forbes Park where the wealthy residents live).

Of all the unlikely things that have happened to me in my entire life, one of the weirdest is when I was invited to a party at a house in Forbes Park. I still believe it was a case of mistaken identity. They apparently thought I was an important person! The sequence of events began when I received an engraved invitation at the hotel inviting me to a dinner at General somebody-or-other's house. I had no idea who this general was, and not the faintest idea why I would be invited. So, I took the invitation to work and showed it to Manny Cu. Manny's reaction was,

"How in the hell did you get that? I've lived in Manila all my life and never got invited to one of those things!'

"Well, should I go?

"Yes, by all means you should go. You don't turn down an invitation like that. I know people who would give almost anything to get invited."

"Who is this guy?"

"He's one of the top officers in the Philippine Air Force. I think he's the second in command. Anyway, he's really close to the Marcos crowd."

The Marcos connection of course referred to Ferdinand Marcos who was the president of the Philippines at that time. After I had thought it over for a while, I started to wonder what I should wear, so I asked Manny about that, too. He said he would get me the proper outfit and sure enough, he did. It was the formal Philippine suit, all white, with the fancy ruffled shirt, open collar. They call that shirt a barong tagalog. The jacket has very wide lapels and large, elegant cuffs. Altogether it is a very sharp looking outfit.

When I replied to the invitation, specifying that I was not bringing anyone else, the lady who was handling it said they would send a car to the hotel to pick me up. At the appointed time, I was waiting at the front of the lobby all dressed up. A blue Air Force Mercedes pulled up, the uniformed driver opened the door to the back seat, and I got in. Surprise! There was a girl sitting there. *"I am your escort for tonight."*

Well, that was a shock. Of course, it didn't take long to figure out that this is the way they treat VIP's. It was just that an old farm boy like me isn't used to things like that. When we got to the house in Forbes Park the, driver opened the door and a servant greeted us and directed us into a big room. The General was shaking hands with all the men as they entered. I noticed that while he was shaking hands with me, he was looking over my shoulder to see who was next. The affair turned out to be a cocktail party with buffet. There was an immense quantity of food, all of which was delicious.

Very soon I learned two things about my escort. First, she had about as much personality as a department store mannequin, and second, she considered it to be her job to hang on to me constantly. Since she wasn't worth a darn for conversation, and she dung to my arm as though she was afraid to let me go, I did not enjoy her companionship very much. Early on, a very pretty and friendly Filipina spotted me and dragged her husband, an American Air Force major, over to meet me. She spoke English without any accent and took care of introductions. Her husband seemed to be a nice guy. All I remember of him is that he was from Texas. Before long, she introduced me to several other couples, who greeted me politely and then went on to talk to somebody else. I mentally classified them as banker types. Sometime during the evening, she introduced me to a classy-looking lady who was friendly and wanted to talk. I had a very interesting conversation with her. She said that she was an architect, and that she was working on the project of restoring the old walled city of Manila. I liked both her looks and her personality. After she wandered off, I managed to ask the major's wife who she was.

"She is the First Lady's cousin."

That really impressed me. At that time there was no doubt that Imelda Marcos, the first lady, was the most famous lady in the Philippines. Almost every day you could see her picture in the newspaper, often on the front page.

Most of the time while I was at the party, I was pretty uncomfortable. The only exceptions were the moments when I was talking to the major or his wife or the Marcos cousin. I knew I didn't belong there, and I felt like most of the guests knew it too. Of course, the fact that I had this bimbo surgically attached to my arm didn't help either. I couldn't help noticing that most of the women we were introduced to would politely acknowledge the introduction then ignore her as though she wasn't there. Obviously, they knew how she fit into the scheme of things. I think the only time she turned me loose during the whole evening was when she went to the comfort room. That is the Philippine euphemism for what we call the restroom. After what seemed to be an appropriate length of time, I let my escort know that I was ready to leave. In a few minutes we went out to find the Mercedes waiting for us. Back in the car my escort dropped a few hints that it was still early and we could go party, but I played dumb. Frankly, I didn't care what she thought of me. Partying with her struck me as a stupid idea, so we went back to the hotel and I said goodnight to her. It was a relief

On our one Sunday off, Manny Cu assigned his car and driver to take Jim Schmidt and me up into the mountains of Luzon. It was a wonderful trip. We drove for a considerable distance, first through rice paddies then groves of mangoes and other fruits. As we gained altitude the mangoes and papayas gave way to banana plantations and forests of coconuts. Our destination was a river village from which we were to take a boat trip into the mountains to a waterfall. In preparation for this excursion, we had been warned to take a swimsuit and t-shirt.

When we reached a village on the bank of a fast-flowing river, we stopped at the house of a couple that handled the arrangements for the canoe trip. Their house, while small, was bright and cheery and spotlessly clean. We changed into our swim gear in their house and boarded a sturdily built narrow wooden boat. The two of us sat in the middle of the boat. The two boatmen took up their positions at the ends. We had already noticed powerboats that were cruising up and down the river pulling a long rope that the boatmen in canoes like ours grabbed to hitch a ride upstream against the strong current. Paddling out to midstream, our boatmen grabbed a towrope, and we were on our way. As we moved upstream, we passed the mouths of tributaries flowing out of the jungle, and after a few miles the channel narrowed as we left the foothills and entered the mountains.

At that point, we dropped the towrope, and the powerboat turned back down stream to make another run to pick up some more tourists. From there on the boatmen paddled. While they were small men, they were incredibly strong and made steady progress. Soon we were threading our way through big rocks. The gorge grew deeper and narrower until we could see only a sliver of sky far above, and in spots we could not see the sky at all because of overhanging rock cliffs and jungle growth. Estimating the height of the sheer rock walls was difficult, but I am sure that we were in a crack in the rocks only about thirty feet wide and at least 600 ft. deep. It was dark in the gorge. I attempted to take a few pictures but did not have a flash so there was not enough light for a picture. Soon we encountered rapids where the boatmen jumped out and scrambling from rock to rock pulled the boat with a short rope. I thought perhaps we would have to get out and walk as well, but they wanted us to stay in the boat. It would have been quite dangerous for us to attempt to negotiate the slippery rocks as our boatmen did.

Finally, the gorge opened into a pool, perhaps the size of two football fields, with a waterfall at the far end. The water fell over a sheer cliff at least as high as a six-story building. In turning the falls into a tourist attraction, the local people arranged a ride through the falls. To do this, they had anchored a large rope to the rock wall at the back of the cave that the turbulent water had carved out at the base of the falls. It was a heavy rope about two inches in diameter. The other end of the rope was anchored in the rocks at the outlet of the pool. They had a raft made of large bamboo lashed together with ropes to carry those who were brave (or foolish) enough to go through the falling water.

A young Australian honeymoon couple had arrived just before us. There was another Filipino at the pool that tended the raft while our boatmen rested. He instructed us men to take off our t-shirts and kneel on the raft. The girl did not want to try the raft trip, but the raft tender would not take no for an answer. So, she finally gave in and joined the other three of us plus the raft tender on the raft. The rafts man secured himself with a loop of rope, grabbed the heavy rope, and pulled us hand over hand toward the falls. He had told us to hang on tight to the ropes that held the raft together. The water below the falls was incredibly rough. It would have been impossible to keep from being thrown from the raft had we not been clinging to the ropes. As we approached the falls, we were first drenched by spray, then the full force of the water hit us. The weight of the water was immense. All I could do was hang on with all my might as the water twisted, turned, and vibrated my body. After what seemed like a long distance we emerged into the spray and water drips in the cave under the falls. As soon as she could get her breath the girl began screaming. Her bikini top had come off! As a matter of fact, if we had not been in the kneeling position, we all might have lost our swimsuits! Meanwhile, the rafts man was laughing his head off. Finally, it dawned on me why he had been so insistent on getting the girl on the raft.

The ride back out of the cave was uneventful. Making a big swing to the side, we avoided the main falls and the rough water. The ride down through the gorge was a thrill. We shot through the rocky channel at hair-raising speed. At times the boatman in the front was doing a display of acrobatics that was almost like a ballet dance. Time after time, as we were careening through the maze of rocks, we were headed for what looked like an unavoidable crash. At precisely the right moment he would do a handstand on the boat, throw his body horizontally and push us away from the rock with his legs, only to make an equally spectacular save only a few seconds later.

Returning to the house where we changed clothes again, we drove back to the city by a different route. The roads were narrow and crooked. When you rounded a curve, you never knew when there might be people walking in the roadway or a carabao (water buffalo) that saw no reason why he should get out of the way. On our way back to the city, we stopped in a coconut grove where a couple of natives demonstrated how they harvest the coconuts growing sixty feet or more from the ground.

Back on the job in Manila, we had a few minor skirmishes with the immigration bureaucrats because we were staying longer than we had originally predicted. Alan Frazer distributed a little grease money in the right places to take care of that problem. By this time the people at Pacific Data Corporation were quite familiar with our requirements and were doing a good job. Jim Schmidt and I felt that they did not need us anymore, so we wound up our work and flew back to Denver by way of Los Angeles.

36

The Eighties

I can't remember just when it was that Arlene and I got concerned that Dave was getting close to the deadline for finishing his PHD thesis. He had completed the work that went into it at the University of Illinois before he went to work in California, but he still had to finish the thesis before he could get his degree. After he went to work, he didn't do much on it for quite a while, and there was a real danger he wouldn't get it completed and would lose all the time and hard work he had put in. I took two weeks of vacation, flew to California, and did whatever I could to help him get it done. His boss let him take a couple of weeks to work on it and gave him the use of a conference room as well as the services of one of the secretaries to type. He did all the hard work. I just edited for correct cross-references, punctuation, and grammatical errors. By the time I left, the thesis was ready to send in for approval. I know it went back and forth two or three more times before all the nit-picking details were taken care of and it was finally accepted just a few hours before the deadline. He finally got his PHD degree. What a relief!

David and Marilyn were married about that time too. They first set up house in San Juan Capistrano, and I visited them several times there when I went to California on business. Laine, our oldest granddaughter, was born there.

Early on, we decided to stay in the house on Sylvia Drive even though it was where we lost Paul. I think both of us had the feeling that it would be like unfinished business if we left there right away. I think we both still feel it was the right decision. We had some very good years there while Kristen was growing up. She had a lot of fun playing with the other kids in the neighborhood. When we finally were ready to move, Kristen was going into junior high. We wanted her to go to Huron Junior High, and we were glad to find a good new house on Claire Lane. When we made the move, there was no problem leaving Sylvia Drive. It was just another chapter in our lives, and it was time to close the chapter. We moved to Claire Lane in May 1980.

Arlene was having more and more symptoms that indicated she might have serious heart problems. In 1982, she had bypass surgery, requiring two bypasses. She has had a lot more trouble with blockage since then. She quit teaching about that time and has never worked outside the home since, except for volunteer work of Kristen's school and church.

David transferred from California to Tulsa, Oklahoma, where he worked for Cities Service. Arlene, Kristen, and I went to Tulsa a time or two while they lived there.

My situation at work was changing too. I was still a manager in charge of a programming group but working on different applications and new equipment. While I had worked on IBM mainframes for my entire career except for a very short time at the very beginning when I did a little work on an old Univac, I now had to learn the care and feeding of a new breed of hardware, the huge and cranky water-cooled Sperry-Univac. I went to school once again to learn the language we had to use. I went to another school to learn enough about the hardware to design applications for it. In theory, the Sperry Univac design was superior in many ways to IBM, but in practice, we found ourselves testing unproven designs in a high-volume production environment and dealing with an inadequate service force. Those machines were still in use when I left the company, but the manufacturer went through a chaotic period of mergers and buyouts, which made an already shaky position much worse. From my personal point of view, my Sperry-Univac training was a waste of time. Actually, my programming group worked on applications for the IBM, too.

During my entire career with Mountain Bell, the company was part of the highly structured and predictable universe of AT&T. The process of continuing education never stopped. I went to many different technical schools and completed quite a number of management courses as well. While I never graduated from college, I strongly feel that by the time my Bell System career ended I had earned the equivalent of a bachelor's degree or better in my field. We worked closely with Bell Labs and the training and technical assistance organizations within AT&T. I did a lot of traveling for the company, most of it within the Mountain Bell area, but also many trips to New Jersey and more than a few to such places as Chicago, New York, Atlanta, Seattle, San Francisco, and Los Angeles. I spent so much time in Salt Lake City I felt like I had a second office there. Many of my fellow workers did a hitch in New Jersey, usually three years working for Bellcore, Bell Labs or AT&T. I had opportunities to do that too, but always declined.

There was one slightly insane opportunity that I did volunteer for and I am thankful that I did not get it. During the last few years of the reign of the Shah of Iran, AT& T contracted with the Iranian government to build a brand-new telephone System in Iran. When the time came to staff the programming force for this project, AT&T screened the records of the Bell System to find people who had the required skills and sent hundreds of letters to programming groups where there were possible candidates. Ozell and I were both on the list, as were many of the old-timers in our department. He and I discussed it, at first almost as a joke, and then more seriously. We decided what the heck; let's go for it.

That started the wheels turning. Nancy and Arlene even talked about how they could travel while Ozell and I worked there. In the course of time, both Ozell and I were notified that we had passed the preliminary screening, and we could expect to be scheduled for all the preparatory work that had to be done. That was precisely the time when the revolution in Iran exploded. The Shah was thrown out, the Americans in Iran had to flee on a few hours notice, and those who did not escape were held hostage. That is a perfect example of the truth of the old adage, *"Be careful what you wish for-- you might get it!"*

Ozell had probably been under more pressure to go to work in New Jersey than I ever was, and he eventually decided to go. He was spending a lot of time working there anyway. If I remember correctly, he went to work for Bellcore in Piscataway, NJ, late in 1983. The Roberts moved to Bridgewater, NJ. I made it a point to visit at their house if I had the opportunity whenever I was in New Jersey. That happened two or three times, because by that time I was spending a good deal of time there myself. Arlene, Kristen, and I also made a vacation trip out there.

The storm clouds that foretold the breakup of the Bell System were gathering. In 1983 the famous decision was handed down, and the date was set: January 1, 1984. Almost immediately, older employees started retiring in droves. They were encouraged to do so by the offering of a series of incentive plans. I was a little short of the required length of service to get the maximum benefits, so I had to stay a little longer. For years I had planned to retire when I had 30 years of service but after completing 26 years, the end was near. I was now an employee of US West. The work atmosphere had been getting tense and unpredictable during the last days of Mountain Bell, and with the formation of US West, it got a lot worse. For me, personally, it was obvious that they were trying to push me out the door. Finally, in the spring of 1985 the company announced another retirement plan that fit my age and length of service. I jumped at the opportunity and on May 30, 1985, I retired.

Ozell retired the same day I did. The coincidence was complete. We started at almost the same time, we worked in the same locations most of the time and we retired from US West with almost the same length of service. He and Nancy had decided to retire in Las Cruces, New Mexico, so they moved directly from New Jersey to Las Cruces.

Free from the obligation of going to work every day for the first time in my life, except for short vacations, I stayed home and worked at finishing the landscaping of our yard.

When I retired from US West in 1985, I really had no intention of ceasing work altogether. It took me a couple of months to catch up with the backlog of work in and around the house, but before long I got serious about looking for a job. It was discouraging at first because there were a lot of people who retired from the former Bell System companies at about the same time. I soon found that while there were some jobs available for people with my qualifications, there were many applicants for every job.

That was the situation in July of 1985 when I walked into the Denver office of National Exchange Carriers Association, a company that was formed at the time of the breakup of the Bell System to handle some of the financial work that had been formerly been done by AT&T. The consent decree specifically prohibited AT&T from handling certain funds. NECA was hurriedly thrown together to do the job.

In talking with the manager of the Denver NECA office I soon found that they had no need for a person with my skills in Denver, but that they were looking for such a person in the headquarters in Whippany, New Jersey. Right then and there he called NECA data systems in Whippany and very quickly I was connected to Frank Bruczinski who managed the systems development and maintenance group. Frank and I talked for a while and he offered to pay for a trip to New Jersey to interview for a job.

The idea of going to work in New Jersey after retirement had never occurred to me before. Before divestiture, when Mountain Bell was still part of the Bell System, many of the people from our department went to New Jersey for three-year hitches. I had several opportunities to do that in the last few years I worked for Mountain Bell, but I never was interested. In fact, when Ozell Roberts was transferred there, I emphatically stated that I was not going to

follow him, as I had in all his previous moves within the company. Now the picture was completely different. I had a powerful incentive to make the jump, because I still had house payments to make, and I knew I had to have additional income. After that I went home and dropped the bombshell--I was considering a job in New Jersey!

Arlene agreed that it was worth a try. We agreed from the outset that we would not all move. Kristen was in high school and we had no intention of making her change schools. After a few more phone calls, the NECA people agreed to buy me a plane ticket to come out for an interview. Once again, as I had so many times before, I flew to Newark. The interview went well, and they offered me a job with benefits and a substantial raise in pay over what I had been making at US West. I accepted.

37

New Jersey

Back home, I had to decide what I couldn't get along without, and then figure out how to pack it all into my Mustang, which didn't have a lot of space for anything. With every inch of the Mustang stuffed full, I set out for New Jersey. The Mustang was used when I bought it, and it had been driven a lot of miles. However, it was still a good car. I had never driven it on a long trip until I went to New Jersey. All was well until I got to Joliet, IL, near Chicago on the second day. Something went wrong with the rack-and-pinion steering box, and the car became very hard to steer. I managed to limp into a motel and locate a shop nearby. That cost me a day, but since I had allowed plenty of time for the trip it didn't matter. The rest of the trip was uneventful.

I had to live in motels for over two weeks before I found a furnished room in a home in Madison, NJ about five miles from my job. Both owners were professors at a college almost next door to their home.

My title was Manager, Application Development. In most respects, the job turned out to be almost the same thing I had been doing in Denver. The major difference was that I was assembling a larger group of programmers than I had ever supervised in Mountain Bell or US West. As a part of my duties, I interviewed job candidates and decided whom to hire. That part of the job was completely new to me. Before long, I had so many people reporting to me that I had no time for doing any programming myself. I had always done some programming at Mountain Bell. At NECA, the only hands-on technical work I did occasionally was to help a programmer when he or she encountered a particularly elusive bug. I found that I was the only person in the group that would attempt to read a core dump. There were so many debugging tools available by that time that an application programmer really didn't need to know how do it the hard way. I got some satisfaction from knowing that while all my employees had more formal education than I did, there were still problems I could handle that they could not.

At NECA my job was management, period. I always had seven or eight programmers and analysts in my group and at times I had as many as 11 contractors besides. One reason the job was fun was that the people on the management staff were all very experienced and knew their jobs well. In the beginning most of them were concerned only with getting the job done and were glad to leave the corporate politics in their home companies behind. Some were retirees like me. Most of them were on loan from the Baby Bells, GTE, and a bunch of other independent telephone companies. Our parking lot looked like a tourist trap with license plates from most of the 50 states. Most people did as I did, keeping their cars licensed in their home state at least for a while. That reflected the prevailing belief that the NECA job was not permanent, and most of us would eventually go home.

Arlene came out to stay with me now and then, and I went home occasionally. She managed very well in Northglenn without me. Kristen was happy in school, so I didn't have to worry much about them. I started to look for a house to buy almost immediately. I came awfully close to buying two different places before Arlene came out and went house hunting with me. She immediately picked out Panther Valley as her first-choice area. I had been leaning toward another condominium development on the other side of Hackettstown, but she liked a condo in Panther Valley better, and we bought it. Either way I was looking at a long commute to work, but it was impossible to find anything close to work that we could afford. As it turned out it was a very good buy. We had the cheapest unit in a very pretty upscale neighborhood with a beautiful golf course. I am not a golfer, but I like golf course neighborhoods. I spent a few Saturdays going to garage sales and before long furnished the condo, mostly with the stuff I picked up.

Soon after I moved into the condo, I went to a service in the Panther Valley Community church. I sat near the back. As soon as the service was over, a lady who was sitting directly ahead of me turned around and said,

"You ought to sing in the choir."

She literally took me by the arm and escorted me to meet the choir director. That choir practiced right after the service every Sunday, so I practiced right then and there. Although I never joined the church, I sang with the choir whenever I was in town from that time until I moved away. Arlene came with me and sang too when she was there. The choir people were the only ones I ever really knew in that church, but I enjoyed singing with them and going to the choir parties. The director was a music professor in a little church college. He loved a-cappella singing so we usually sang without accompaniment or with only a guitar. He also was very interested in 15th century church music, and every now and then he would throw one of those pieces at us. I remember trying to find my way through Xerox copies of very old handwritten manuscripts written in the original French or German. If there was a translation, it often didn't fit very well. In fact, usually we just did our best to try to sing the song in the original language. It was a good thing he was tolerant of our mistakes!

During one of her first trips to New Jersey after I moved into the condo, Arlene got very sick. She was in terrible pain, but we really didn't know what was causing it. She had been sick before she left home, but doctors there didn't seem to be able to diagnose what was wrong. At the Hackettstown hospital, they took a while to diagnose it too, but decided it was gall bladder and operated to remove it. They found it so badly infected it was about ready to burst. It was a tough surgery, but she recovered quite fast. We found that Hackettstown had a good hospital and good doctors.

We hung some wallpaper in the condo and bought a new sofa and it was really a pretty good little place to live. Snow removal was a big problem in the winter, and we could hear the guy in the next unit banging his exercise equipment, but those were relatively minor annoyances.

My turn at getting sick came a little later. I had one urinary infection after another. One doctor was delighted to tell me I had prostate cancer, but I got a second opinion. I went into the Hackettstown hospital for a biopsy. That turned into a terrible ordeal. I was living alone at the time. The biopsy was supposed to be a very minor day surgery, so I drove to the hospital. They turned me loose with a catheter. I couldn't drive so I had to take a cab home and leave my car at the hospital. I was stuck at home, in constant pain. I don't know what I would have done without my friend Joe Mecca and his wife Nancy. They came and brought me a little food and retrieved my car and visited every night to make sure that I had something to eat. After a week of constant pain, I removed the catheter myself and drove to the doctor's office, which was in Newton about 25 miles from my house.

The good news was that I didn't have cancer. The bad news was that I had to have prostate surgery. Arlene came out to stay while I had the surgery and recovered. The surgery was painful, but not as bad as the biopsy had been. Unfortunately, twelve days after the surgery I developed some complications and I had to go back to the hospital in the middle of the night and have more surgery. I was laid up for weeks, not even able to ride in the car.

I missed the singing I had been doing with the chorale in Colorado, so I immediately started looking for a singing group when I moved to New Jersey. I visited a couple of barbershop chapters but didn't feel like I really fit in although they made me welcome. A lady who was working as a contractor at NECA happened to mention that she sang with the Masterwork Chorus, based in Morristown, NJ. They were practicing for the Christmas season, when they traditionally sang Handel's Messiah in many different locations. I have always said that I got into Masterwork by the back door. While the chorus was strictly limited to 88 regular members, they always brought in more singers for the Messiah. The Masterwork Chorus is an old group with a fine reputation. For many years they have had a waiting list of singers who would like to join. My co-worker invited me to a practice session. I did not audition, although the director made me sit in the front row right in front of him so he could hear. I remember that he asked me at the end of the rehearsal if I had any trouble with the music. I replied truthfully that I did. Apparently, that was what he wanted to hear, for he allowed me to come back every week and sing in the bass section. I sang in the Messiah performances in New Jersey that year but did not go to the big ones in New York City. After the Christmas season was over, nobody said anything to me one way or the other about continuing with the group, although I knew they were very selective as to whom they admitted into membership. I just kept going to practice.

That spring the chorus was renting an old unused elementary school building in Mendham, NJ, for practice and also subletting some of the classrooms for music lessons. The walls of the big old all-purpose room where the chorus practiced were very dirty, so the chorus decided to paint it. The president asked for volunteers, and I signed up. The lady who was appointed committee chairman took care of getting paint, ladders and all the other stuff we needed. She planned to do it on a Saturday, but when the day arrived, she and I were the only people who showed up. We went ahead anyway and spent the whole weekend hard at work. We rolled on 18 gallons of paint! We did a good job, too.

All the time I had been with Masterwork I had been sitting in the back trying to attract as little attention as possible. At the next rehearsal after we painted the room, the president of the chorus approached me at break and after thanking me for the work said:

"You have never auditioned."

"No."

"Come with me."

She took me to one of the classrooms where there was a piano, found an accompanist and put me through an audition. When it was over, she said, "*You're in.*"

That was the way I was admitted into membership in the Masterwork Chorus. After that I sang with them in quite a few concerts, including five in Avery Fisher Hall in the Lincoln Center in New York, and four in Carnegie Hall.

Meanwhile, Kristen was doing fine in high school. She played in the band for a while and enjoyed her high school years. I was still working in New Jersey when she graduated, so I had to make a quick trip home for her graduation. Arlene managed quite well without me, although we spent a lot of time on the phone.

During this time the personal computer became a necessary part of our lives. The Internet had not yet emerged from its gestation period and was not available to the public, but software and modems were available to dial up a connection between computers and send files over the phone line. Kristen and I had mastered that technique before I went to New Jersey, but we each had to buy a PC to make it work. Within a month or so after I got there, I had my new PC and from that time forward we sent a lot of stuff back and forth. She always wanted me to look at her English papers before she handed them in. We continued to do this after she went to the University of Arizona.

She went into a business information system major, which of course involved a good deal of programming, and I helped with that. I even helped her roommate with a few programs, but it soon became obvious that the roommate was quite happy to let me write her programs, so she didn't have to, so I had to start refusing. Kristen graduated Cum Laude from the U of A, and I like to think that I can claim a little credit for her success, because when it came to writing, I was probably her severest critic. I did a tough job of grading her papers before she turned them in. Of course, she had a good background in high school before she went to the University. Northglenn High School did an excellent job of preparing students for college.

As I started the third year of my hitch at NECA, things were not going as well as they had the first two years. By that time, I had reported to two different immediate supervisors, both of whom were technical types, and we had gotten along quite well. My experience with the third was a different story. He came from New Jersey Bell, just a few miles from where NECA was located. In all fairness, I will have to say that he must have been a good employee at one time, or he never would have been promoted to a middle management level. However, from what I learned from former associates, his drinking had progressed to the point where he was a problem to everyone around him and an embarrassment to the company. Anyway, Bell Atlantic, the Baby Bell successor to New Jersey Bell, solved their problem by loaning him to NECA, where conveniently enough his boss was an old friend from New Jersey Bell. Working for him was awful. When he was drunk, he was completely unreasonable, and when he was hung over, he was mean and bad-tempered. The best times at the office were when he was absent. Quite often he would get drunk at lunch and then shut the door of his office and sleep.

Though, one of his demands turned out to be a blessing in disguise for me. After one of the other managers quit, my boss told me to take care of his group until they found a replacement. That was okay. That group staffed the help desk and took daily telephone reports from all the regional offices in 50 states, Puerto Rico, and the Virgin Islands. The people who manned the phones knew their jobs and could handle everything without getting me involved. All I really had to do was plan the schedule, check the time sheets, and make sure that someone was available to answer the phone.

The hard part was my boss's edict that I had to be there whenever any of my people were in the building. Of course, I still had my regular group, thirteen of them, and now the extra six. The programming group worked staggered hours to use our computer time to the fullest, and the phone desks were scheduled to cover all the time zones. That meant that my workday started a 6:00 AM when St. Thomas in the

Virgin Islands started their daily report and ended at 8:30 PM when Honolulu, Hawaii finished their report. Including a half-hour for lunch that added up to 14 1/2 hours every day. All through my career I was often called on to work that long or longer in a day when necessary, but to be forced to do it day in and day out when there was really no need was a different story. To make matters worse, I had to drive an hour each way in the dark going to and from work.

The temporary arrangement lasted longer than I expected. I began writing programs in the evening when I got tired of doing my regular work, and that was good because I had stopped programming completely when I retired from US West. When I left NECA, I was much better prepared for consulting work because of those enforced review sessions.

As I mentioned before, most of the people who started NECA were on loan from AT&T, the Baby Bells, and GTE. Some of the managers carried over into NECA the paternalistic attitude and the emphasis on long-term employment that was such a strong element of the philosophy of the Bell System. That management style was doomed to die in the post-divestiture world, but while it persisted, the effect could be either good or bad. At best, it provided a place where good people could continue to contribute even though they were being forced out of their home companies because of changes in management and corporate downsizing. At worst, it turned this upstart company into a dumping ground for misfits. Being deprived of their sheltered environment, most of these problem employees could not stand the pressure and did not stay long.

I left NECA in February 1988. That was six months short of the three years I had agreed to work there, but their policy permitted that much flexibility. There was no problem in selling the condo. It sold eleven days after I listed it, and I made a neat profit. Arlene and I took the long way home, down through Virginia, Washington, D. C., the Carolinas, to Savannah, Georgia, then meandered back home from there. We stopped for a little while at Rock Island, IL, to see

Arlene's sister Jeanette and her husband Merle Carlson. I have always been glad we did because Merle was dying of cancer and passed away a month later.

38

Home Again

Back home in Northglenn, I was unemployed for a little while, but soon got started on another career as a consultant, doing contract programming. I worked for several different consulting companies at different times, some of them more than once, depending on what skills they needed at the moment. For the most part, I enjoyed the work, and even when I was on an assignment I didn't particularly like, it was not terribly stressful because I always knew it would end soon and I would go on to the next job. I went from one employer to the next, and one assignment to the next, without much interruption. Two weeks was about the longest time I ever had between jobs. With the money I made on the condo and the good wages I made as a consultant, we were able to pay off the house on Claire Lane, and for the first time in 30 years we did not have to make a house payment.

After a few years of retirement, Ozell and Nancy moved from Las Cruces back to the Denver area because of his declining health. He had a few relatively good years in Las Cruces and enjoyed fishing, boating and golf. Nancy taught at the University of Texas at El Paso for a while. However, his polycystic kidneys were getting progressively worse, and they needed to be closer to good medical facilities. Their kids Mike and Kim also lived in this area, so they wanted to be near them too. They had a little house in Thornton that they had bought some years before. That gave them a place to live until they found a bigger one, they liked and moved even closer to us. Almost immediately, Ozell had to go on dialysis. By that time, he was very sick. Despite heroic efforts to prolong his life, the polycystic kidney disease eventually killed him. He and Nancy were married for 39 years. He had become part of our family, and we missed him a great deal. We remember the good times and have stayed close friends with Nancy and their kids who are part of our extended family.

39

Empty Nest

We are empty nesters now. Most of the significant events in our lives now concern the children and grandchildren. Cheryl got divorced. That was a terribly stressful time for her and her boys, David, and Scott, as well as for us, especially Arlene. We made some extra trips to Tucson to help her move and furnish what support we could. We have traveled the road to Tucson many times since then. Despite the hardships of being a single mom and working at a demanding job that doesn't pay a big salary, she has done a fine job of raising the boys, David, and Scott.

Kristen went to work in Houston for Shell Oil immediately after she graduated. That job lasted only about a year before she was laid off. She and Steve Valdez were married in 1991. He was working in Dallas at the time, and she was in Houston. They soon moved to Indianapolis, where they both went into programming. Kristen has worked with student loans, and Steve has been consulting in many different applications.

Kristen and Steve bought a new house in Fishers, Indiana, after they had been there a while. Both Kaitlyn and Sedona were born while they lived in that house. I have been called upon to do little jobs in their house whenever we visit. I always enjoy those tasks. Since then, they had a big new house custom built. It is a beautiful place in a newer part of Fishers.

Our son David (with a son and grandson both named David I have to be explicit) left Occidental Petroleum and transferred from California to Tulsa, Oklahoma, working for Cities Service. Three years after Laine's birth, they had another girl, Leah. He moved from Tulsa to Plano, Texas, working for Arco. They stayed in Plano until 1991, when he was transferred to Anchorage, Alaska.

Their youngest, Mark was born in Anchorage. That gave us a good excuse to go to Alaska. We have thoroughly enjoyed every trip we have made up there. We took a tour the first time we were there, making a big circle from Anchorage to Whittier by bus and train, then by boat to Valdez, then by bus the rest of the way to Fairbanks, Denali, and back to Anchorage. We went there once in the winter, too, staying with the grandchildren while Dave and Marilyn went to California, and spending Thanksgiving with them.

Shortly after I turned 65, I gave up consulting work. At that time Social Security imposed an earnings limit for each year. If you exceeded that amount, Social Security demanded that their payments for the rest of the year be paid back. I found that even one contract a year was enough to push me over the limit. My birthday is in December, and I start receiving Social Security payments at the first of the following year. I was able to stay into the next year on my current contract until I hit the earnings limit, and then I gave up computer work altogether. I didn't work at all for the rest of that year.

For the first time in my life, I had to try to adjust to really being retired, not just being in-between jobs. I went through the rest of the year without looking for anything else, but as soon as January 1, 1994, rolled around I started looking for a retirement job. I found one soon afterward, delivering flowers for the Center Greenhouse retail store and florist. It was fun. The Yantomo family, whom we had known through our church for a long time, owns the greenhouse. Paul Yantomo, one of the partners in the business at that time, is the son-in-law of my good friend Darrell Schroeder. Darrell had retired from his insurance agency and gone to work for the greenhouse a couple of years before and was their truck driver. Delivering their products was a seasonal job and fit my situation perfectly. At first, I worked for both the retail and wholesale departments but after a year, they phased out the retail business and I went over to the wholesale side. The Yantomos were great people to work for. I worked three months of the year driving a truck on both local and regional deliveries. In the spring the company rented extra trucks to keep up with the seasonal demand, so I drove a variety of different makes of diesels with 24-ft. van bodies. I enjoyed driving those trucks. The trip I enjoyed the most was the run up 1-70 over the mountains to Vail and sometimes to Aspen. In the late spring and early summer, I often made that run five times a week. I finished the spring delivery season in June of 1998 but was then forced to give up that truck-driving job because of health problems.

40

European Tour

In 1995 Arlene and I went on a tour of Europe. We flew to Frankfurt, where we joined a tour group. We traveled by bus for two weeks. We had an excellent tour guide and a very congenial group of fellow travelers. We did not know any of them when we started, but it didn't take long to make friends.

There were many high points on the tour. We toured Germany from Frankfurt south into Switzerland, visited several places in Switzerland, made a very short excursion into France and another into Italy, just long enough to say we'd been there, then on to Austria, then back through Germany. It is hard to say which place we liked the best, but Innsbruck, Austria was a favorite.

During the tour we learned a great many facts about the countries we visited, but some of the things we remembered best were simply impressions. I was very interested in Switzerland because of my family heritage. Swiss people are not unfriendly but are quite reserved in their dealings with foreigners. The German speaking part of Switzerland is extraordinarily orderly, neat, and clean, truly like a picture postcard. The Swiss don't seem to have very much fun, though. Life in Switzerland is lived with military precision. The military analogy is very appropriate for as the saying goes: "*Switzerland does not have an army, Switzerland is an army*".

Every able-bodied man in Switzerland must serve his time on active duty with the army and then be in the active reserve for many years. The reservists do not leave their military responsibilities when they go home. They keep their uniform, rifle, and a box of ammunition in their home, so they are ready to defend their country on very short notice. The whole country is heavily fortified although the fortifications are so well concealed that tourists are usually not aware of them at all.

Another characteristic of the country is the noticeable differences in the cantons (what they call the 26 states of Switzerland). Canton Glarus, ancestral home of my father's family, retains its autonomy and is still a pure democracy, where through their annual meeting every citizen has a voice in the government. We found Canton Glarus to be intensely interested in preserving its own culture.

How would I describe the Swiss mountain villagers? Hardworking, serious, intelligent, compulsively neat, tough, practical, stubborn, and slow to accept change--these are the attributes that come to mind. They are quite aware that for centuries many of the best and the brightest of their children have been leaving their homeland and making a new life in other countries. At the same time, they acknowledge that while their mountains are beautiful, they are also harsh and unforgiving and cannot support a large population.

After we left the tour at Frankfurt, we traveled by train back to Switzerland. Those trains are nice, but when we rode on the local train from Zurich to Glarus, we found the journey a little difficult because they did not announce the stops. When you get on or off those trains, you must move fast. At the local stops in Switzerland, they stop only 30 seconds or less. I timed most of the stops at 28 seconds. Since they did not announce the stops, I had to use my map and watch for the station signs to determine where we were and when it was time to get ready to get off.

My grandparents came from the village of Engi, located in a high mountain valley a few miles from the town of Glarus, which is the capitol of the canton of Glarus. We made our headquarters at a hotel in Glarus for the week we were there. We only went to the little village of Engi once. We probably should have spent more time there, but we covered it thoroughly considering the short time we visited there. While in most of Europe many people speak English, making it relatively easy for an American to communicate, the people of Engi speak only a few words of English at best. Most of them speak no English at all.

We took the postal bus from Glarus to Engi. We got off the bus and proceeded to walk through the town, which lies at the base of a steep mountain and faces an equally rugged mountainside on the other side of the stream. It was not a long walk from one end to the other, about the equivalent of five city blocks. The main street is the road that intersects with the highway from Glarus and follows a mountain stream a few miles up to Engi, then continues to the head of the valley at the town of Elm. The village of Engi is only three streets wide at its widest point. Some of the dwellings on the edge of town are actually farmhouses, with a barn close by or even attached to the house.

After making inquiries in the only grocery store, we were directed (mostly by gestures) to go to the town hall, which is also the school building. A man and woman in the town office understood us well enough to find out who we were and determine our branch of the Blumer family tree. It took him only a few moments to find the proper page in a big old book and find the record showing when Johannes and Elizabeth Blumer left Engi to go to America. There was only one person in town, an art teacher in the school, who spoke good English. They called her out of the classroom briefly to meet us. Shortly afterward, she took her lunch hour to walk with us through town and tell us about the community. She knew where my great-grandfather's house was. We walked by it and took lots of pictures. It is a very nice house and has been completely renovated. It is apparently in very good condition, even though it is probably at least 250 years old.

Most of the family names in Engi and even those in Glarus were familiar to me. There are Blumers everywhere in that little out of the way corner of Switzerland, and probably even more by the name of Marty, (or Marti, depending on how some ancestor preferred to spell it). My grandmother was a Marty. Arlene has never let me live down the fact that I would not go to the door of a house where one of the Blumer families lived and try to talk to them. I guess I was afraid they would be suspicious of me. We rode the bus to Elm, continuing up the valley to its highest point. Being a ski resort, it is more modern and busier than Engi. There were a number of people from Engi on their way to a funeral and they obviously knew who we were even though none of them spoke English. When we came back from Elm on the bus, the same group was on their way home. There was one older man, very well dressed, who seemed to be a local historian because we could get the drift of what he was telling the others, which was apparently who my family was and when they left Engi and where my family lived in Iowa. That much we could understand, and he obviously knew the facts because he mentioned other family names that were familiar to me because they were ones that I knew from Renwick and LuVerne, Iowa. On the bus ride back to Engi, one older lady tried to talk to us, but all we could get out of it was that she was a Blumer and that her sisters were with her. In any case, there was no doubt that everyone in town knew who we were within two hours. It would have been wonderful if we could have had an interpreter.

Back in Glarus, we found many people that spoke English. We did chat with the owner of the Blumer children's clothing store and sewing shop next door to the hotel in Glarus. We also attempted to connect with the owner of the Blumer computer store, with no luck there. Of course, we noticed the office of Blumer, attorney of law, and the Blumer employment agency.

When we went to the museum at Nafels, near Glarus, we found references to our family name all over the place. In fact, when I went into the portrait gallery, the very first portrait I saw was of one of my ancestors! I know for a fact that I am a direct descendent because he is very prominent in our family tree. One of the branches of the Blumer family-owned textile mills and a part of the museum features the company history and their products. Unfortunately, I came from a poor branch of the family not the branch of the wealthy mill owners. Textiles are still manufactured in Canton Glarus, but the mill in Engi is not in operation. Engi, aside from the old, retired people, is now only the home of a few dairy farmers and a tiny bedroom community for people who work elsewhere.

We found abundant evidence that the Glarners (residents of Glarus) that immigrated to America faced a lot of opposition and ridicule at the time they left. Now, however, the citizens of Canton Glarus point with pride to the successes that those emigrants accomplished in America. One whole section of the museum is devoted to the Glarner Swiss in America. There is a strong implication that those who left were the smart ones, but naturally many of the present residents would not admit the truth of that statement. Perhaps only the present-day residents who have traveled abroad are likely to acknowledge the wisdom of those who chose to emigrate.

After our week in Glarus we returned to Frankfurt for the long flight home. We remember that European tour as one of our favorite vacations.

41

Back in Northglenn, Colorado

We settled back into the old routine. I continued seasonal truck driving for another three years.

1998 was a year to remember, but that doesn't mean that everything that happened that year was good. As soon as the spring planting season was over at the end of June, I was through with my seasonal trucking job for the year. We immediately took a vacation trip to Indianapolis to see Kristen and Steve and the granddaughters, and worked our way back through Illinois and Iowa, visiting relatives along the way. By the time we got to Iowa, I was feeling some pains that I suspected were signals of arterial blockage. I got in to see our cardiologist late in July, and he put me through a treadmill stress test. He went on vacation right afterward, so I didn't get the results for a few days. Arlene had been feeling fine. One Tuesday night I went to chorale practice as usual, and Arlene was out in the backyard fertilizing her flowers. The heart attack hit just as she came in the door. She was able to make it to the phone and call 911. The fire department and ambulance were there in a few minutes, but she had the door locked. She was trying to crawl to the door to open it, but before she got there the next-door neighbor Sherry Perez who had a key rushed over and unlocked the door. The paramedics rushed Arlene to the nearest hospital, St. Anthony North. Sherry Perez found out where I was and came to tell me what had happened. The prompt response probably saved Arlene's life.

I spent a lot of time in the hospital that night and the next day. The second morning after that, I went to see Arlene in the ICU first thing in the morning. I wasn't feeling well. The nurse on duty in the ICU looked at me and told me I had better see a doctor. The first thing I did was go to a payphone and call our cardiologist, Dr. Greenberg. I believe the office nurse I talked to pulled my file and took it to the doctor. Anyway, after a short time she came back on the line and told me to get my butt into their office right away.

Ed Lang, Nancy's friend, took me to Dr. Greenberg's office, which is next to the Aurora South Medical Center close to thirty miles from our house and about 25 from the hospital Arlene was in. Once I got there, they wouldn't let me go home. They rushed me in for an angiogram and as soon as it was done scheduled me for bypass surgery two days later. Not a good coincidence-- both of us with serious heart problems at the same time! Cheryl and my brother Phil and his wife Do Jean came from Arizona to help while we were both unable to do very much. We both made good recoveries and were back to our usual routine quite soon. Our granddaughter Leah came and stayed with us for a while, as did Kristen and Kaitlyn.

The heart trouble episode prompted us to do some serious thinking about moving to a place where we didn't have all the yard work. We were hiring landscapers at the time, which proved to be expensive. The yard was beautiful, but it took a lot of work to keep it up. I had just completed the job of finishing the basement at 1265 Claire Lane within the previous year. That increased the finished area of the house to about 3000 square ft., which was more than we needed. We started looking for condos and townhouses. I looked on the Internet and immediately discovered a townhouse development that I had not previously encountered even though it was very close to where we were living. It is in the Legacy Ridge subdivision. Up to that time we had known Legacy Ridge only as a neighborhood of expensive custom homes. In fact, the Curphys who were long time neighbors of ours in Northglenn had already built a huge custom home and we had visited them in their new place.

We went to look at the model homes and liked one of them very much. After thinking about it for a couple of weeks I brought the subject up again. Arlene liked our home and was not sure she wanted to move, but soon came around to my way of thinking. We signed a contract to buy a townhouse. We expected to wait about ten months before it was built and ready to occupy but the site preparation and construction took 14 months. We decided to list our house for sale in the spring when the yard looked the best.

Construction on our new town home began in May 1999. It was within walking distance of our old house. I soon formed the habit of walking over there almost every day to check on the progress of the building. We took our time choosing a realtor to sell our house and finally chose Patricia Trauernicht, whom we had known for many years. Working with her was a pleasure. The house sold almost immediately. In fact it was sold the first day the listing was announced, and we had a contract by the time the sign was put up in the yard. After all the expenses were paid, we still had enough money left to pay cash for the townhouse and put in all the upgrades and extras we wanted. We set the closing date to be three months after the signing of the contract although we knew we would have to move twice.

Packing, having a big garage sale and just getting rid of things was a big job. After having been in the house for nineteen years we had accumulated a lot of stuff. That house was our home longer than any other place we ever lived. We found a nice one-bedroom apartment reasonably close by and moved when we closed the sale on the old house. Most of our furniture went into storage. We lived in the apartment for three months. It was not a bad experience at all, although it was on the second floor, and both of us had to take our time climbing the stairs. We moved into the townhouse at 2701B W. 106th Loop just before Thanksgiving in 1999. We loved it from the very beginning. It was the right move for us of the right time.

We soon became friends with our closest neighbors, Ken and Mary Allscheid. We took care of their pet bird when they travelled, which we enjoyed. Mary and Ken essentially became extended family as we got to know each other's children and spouses, grandchildren and eventually, great-grandchildren. Later, they gave us a lot of help and support when we got ill and injured.

I had another heart problem early in 2000. Sometime, probably in February, I had a silent heart attack. The cardiologist called it silent because I did not know when it occurred, although I knew that I suddenly became very tired all the time and began having pains that I had not had much since the bypass surgery. I am quite sure that it happened when I was sleeping. I vaguely remember waking up during the night with a severe pain in my left arm, but it soon went away, and I didn't even mention it. More than likely that was when it happened. I also had to start using a CPAP (Continuous Positive Airway Pressure) machine to aid my breathing while sleeping. I have suffered from sleep apnea for a long time. The machine effectively stops the sleep interruptions.

42

Family Happenings

Our big trip in 2000 was when Scott and Laine graduated from high school. There was only a week between Scott's graduation in Tucson and Laine's in Anchorage, Alaska. We drove to Tucson. It was a great day for us when Scott graduated. He had a lot of rough times in school, and there were plenty of times when we could only hope that he would stick with it until he got his diploma. It took a lot of guts for him to go through some of those experiences without giving up. It was a big day for Cheryl, too. Scott's graduation had been one of her goals for a long time. Without her whole-hearted support he probably would never have made it. She threw a big party for him, too, and that was a chance for our family to get together. We really enjoyed it. Considering the precarious state of both Ralph and Amanda's health we learned to appreciate the times that they were both well enough to have a good visit.

Laine's graduation was a high point, of course, but we did a lot of other fun things while we were there. One of the neat things we did on that trip was a day excursion on a boat out of Seward. A humpback whale put on a show for us; and we saw huge flocks of birds and got a good look at a bunch of sea lions. All the guys, except me, went fishing for halibut out of Homer and caught a lot of fish. After they got back to Anchorage, we set up an assembly line in Dave's backyard and packaged filets for freezing, about a hundred pounds worth.

The Glacier, Me, Arlene and David

I went for a solitary walk in the woods every morning and saw moose on three different days, once very close—within about fifteen feet! That is just a little closer than I like to be with a huge wild animal. Another good activity was when we took the Alaska Railroad train to Talkeetna. Arlene and I had been there on our first Alaska trip, but had never ridden the train. I had taken a sightseeing flight out of there on that occasion. The kids wanted to see Mt. McKinley from the air but the weather did not cooperate. It was fine at Talkeetna, but visibility up at Denali was too bad to permit flying. The sightseeing flight service cancelled the flight after waiting a couple of hours for the weather to clear. The train ride that takes you through typical Alaska scenery was fun. On another day, a neighbor who is a pilot gave Laine, Kristen, and Cheryl a sightseeing flight tour for Laine's graduation present. They had a good long flight and got a great look at the country around Anchorage.

Laine started college of the Colorado School of Mines in Golden in the fall of 2000. We helped her move into the dorm and took her back and forth to our house many times during the school year. She liked to come to our house and spend Saturday night and Sunday with us whenever she could.

I went back to work at a different job altogether, working part time for a temporary employee agency. Tempsmart specializes in furnishing hosts and hostesses to work in the sales offices of builders selling new homes. My job was so easy I hesitate to even describe it as work. I would fill in for realtors on their days off, on-site in new home developments, usually where they have model homes. Having worked almost all my life, it was easy to fall back into the routine of going to work. I like to get out of the house and meet people and enjoy the feeling of doing something useful.

2001-2002

Our Golden Wedding Anniversary Party

During the spring of 2001, Kristen and Cheryl started talking about having a party for our golden wedding anniversary in July. It was not that they had any extra time on their hands; Cheryl was working day and night trying to keep up with her job and taking care of Ralph and Amanda who were now almost completely unable to take care of themselves. Nevertheless, they absolutely refused to even consider the possibility of going into assisted living or a nursing home. Kristen and Steve were in the middle of moving. They had a new house built and had to sell their old one and move to an apartment until the new one was finished. They moved into the new house just before they came out to Colorado to celebrate our anniversary.

David and Marilyn were getting ready to move from Anchorage to Bartlesville, Oklahoma too. They were unable to attend our party because he had to be in Bartlesville, and she had to stay in Anchorage to try to sell their house at the same time. However they helped by sharing the cost. Laine was at our house, so she was the only one of that branch of the family who came.

Despite their limited time and the distance involved, the girls did a wonderful job of arranging the party. Nancy, Ed and her kids Mike and Judy and Kim and Stew helped a lot too. We had it at the Westminster Recreation Center. Kristen and Steve made the invitations. Many of our friends mentioned that the invitations were exceptionally good. Cheryl made the table decorations and the two of them made the arrangements with the caterer, Carolyn Vittorelli, who is a member of the Chorale and a friend of mine. Carolyn did a fine job, too. The Chorale dressed up in their best, the women in brand new dresses and the men in their tuxes and sang for half an hour. We estimated that there were about 250-300 guests. Altogether it was a great celebration and went off very smoothly. All of Arlene's surviving brothers and sisters came except Eddie. Our old friends Clarence and Elise Casey came from Iowa too. It was great to visit with them.

Laine is now back at Mines for her sophomore year. We helped her move into a sorority house. It was a lot of hard work! Dave and Marilyn made the big move to Bartlesville, Oklahoma from Anchorage at the same time. Since they moved, we have been able to see them more often and get better acquainted with Mark. He is a computer whiz. All the grandchildren have grown up with computers, but Mark is especially fascinated by them and carries his laptop almost everywhere.

He is carrying on the family tradition by being a good student in school, too. As a matter of fact we are proud of all our grandchildren. They have given us plenty to brag about. We made a big trip to Yakima, Washington in 2002 to attend Leah's graduation. She did her high school work online with the Christa McAuliffe Academy in Yakima and went through high school in three years while living in Portland, Oregon. We were quite impressed by the school. While we were in the Pacific Northwest we went on to Seattle and visited with my nephew Tom Blumer. We have friends in Victoria, British Columbia, so we spent a couple of days in that beautiful city.

2003

During the last year we have lost three members of our extended family. Amanda, wife of my oldest brother Ralph, died. Then Eddie, Arlene's youngest brother passed away, followed by Ralph, all in the space of about eight months. That leaves two of my brothers, and two of Arlene's brothers as well as all four of Arlene's sisters.

None of our children have made any big changes during the last two years, but the young adult grandchildren have. Grandson David got married to Heather O'Hara and they are living in Tucson. David has a good full-time job and is in school at the University of Phoenix. Scott finished Aviation Mechanics School at the top of his class and is now starting Auto Mechanics at Community College while living with his mom Cheryl, working part time, and looking for a "real" job. Laine is now a junior at Mines and living in an apartment. Leah attended Brooks Institute of Photography in Santa Barbara, CA, and then moved to Portland, OR where she is working and going to school to also learn massage therapy. Mark is growing up in Bartlesville where he is the computer guru of his grade in elementary school, but he and Marilyn still like to go back to Anchorage every chance they get. Laine still considers Anchorage to be her home, too. Kristen and Steve's daughters Kaitlyn and Sedona are still little girls but growing up fast and giving

Grandma a good excuse to shop for pretty clothes and toys. Kaitlyn is a first grader and a great little artist. One of her pictures won first prize over hundreds of first grade entries and has been circulated around to many other schools.

2004

Faster than we could have imagined, Laine's four years in college have sped by. She will graduate with a degree in Petroleum Engineering in May 2004. Her wedding is scheduled soon afterward, in June. This year is shaping up to be a high-mileage year for us. We have already driven to Iowa in February to help celebrate the birthday of Arlene's sister Charlotte, who turned seventy in February. We expected the weather to be cold in Iowa, and it was just what we expected. Laine's graduation will be close to our home of course, but we expect to make a trip to Bartlesville anyway. Of course, we will fly to Anchorage for the wedding. It will be nice to see Alaska again.

43

Back to the Land

Throughout this time, we have kept the farm I inherited. It is not the home farm where I grew up, but it is the same land we farmed during the last two years we were in the farming business. The house we lived in and the other buildings are all gone now. In 1982, I sold the house and machine shed to be moved away and hired a contractor to raze all the other buildings. He cut the big trees for logs and bulldozed out and buried everything else. For many years, the land where the buildings once stood has been farmed. The huge cottonwood trees that once were the landmark are only a memory. Even when walking over the place now, it is very difficult to determine where the farmstead once stood. It is good productive farmland that has been easy to keep rented. For at least twenty years now, Randy and Bob Pedersen, sons of our old army friends Pearl and Cecil, have farmed it. They grow only corn and soybeans. Pearl is Arlene's cousin, so we still have a family connection there.

I am still very interested in farming and do whatever is required to manage the landlord's side of the operation. I keep in touch almost daily with what is happening in the business of agriculture. My principal contacts on the Internet are farm people, and the Internet also provides me with price and weather information. Every now and then someone who is an Internet acquaintance drives by our farm and gives me a report on the crops. Even the decorations in my home office carry out the farm theme. I have pictures on the wall of the same models of John Deere and Oliver tractors I once owned, and a scale model of our very first Allis-Chalmers that I first learned to drive. I still regard myself as a farmer at heart.

At the time I am writing this, it is now 2004 and I am 76 years old. It is amazing how much my life and the world I live in have changed since I was a little boy. However, by writing this hodgepodge of narratives I hope I have presented a picture of the way things were at various times. Having written some of the parts of my story as much as 24 years before the last paragraph, it is inevitable that I have repeated references to the same events.

44

Closing The Shutters in 2021

Back row: Terrance Oathout, Marilyn Blumer, Mary Hanson, Kenny Ricklefs, Scott Oathout, Ken Allscheid, David Blumer, David Oathout. Middle row: Kaitlyn Valdez, Mary Allscheid, Bailee and Sedona Valdez, Rylee Oathout, Wuilliam and Laine Valle, Steve Valdez, Heather Oathout. Bottom row: Kristen Valdez, Mark Blumer, Me, Lily Valle, Cheryl Oathout, Zealand Valle

By writing this chronicle, I have done what I could to provide a glimpse of the clutter in my storehouse of memories. It is a personal history, told from my point of view. To bring this up to date, my wife Arlene died on December 30, 2017. Our daughter Kristen and Steve have another daughter, Bailee. Our grandson David and wife Heather had children, Terrance and Rylee Oathout. Our granddaughter Laine married Wuilliam Valle and had Zealand and Lily Valle, twins, and Fridda and Agustin. Grandson Mark Blumer married Sarah Willis. In 2021 I caught COVID-19, after receiving the first vaccine. It made me very sick, but I luckily have recovered and am in a wonderful home receiving round the clock care. Granddaughter Leah Blumer has been visiting me frequently, and helped me publish this book.

In many ways it is impossible to separate the story of my career from the story of my marriage and my family. I hope that the impression I make is that it has been both a good career and a good marriage. Now that the career is over for all practical purposes, I am still left with the memories of a good marriage and a happy and healthy family of which I am proud. I ask for nothing more.

CPSIA information can be obtained
at www.ICGtesting.com
Printed in the USA
BVHW011051180123
656206BV00006B/24/J
* 9 7 8 0 5 7 8 9 1 1 9 5 3 *